Sandra Lee

desserts 2

This book belongs to:

....

Meredith® Books Des Moines, Iowa

Copyright © 2008 Sandra Lee Semi-Homemade® All rights reserved. Printed in the U.S.A.
Library of Congress Control Number 2008922210 ISBN: 978-0-696-24181-9

Brand names identified in this book are suggestions only. The owners of such brand names retain all
right, title, and interest in and to their respective brands. No manufacturers or brand
name owners have endorsed this collection or any recipe in this collection.

Special thanks to Culinary Director Jeff Parker

sem·i·home·made

adj. **1:** a stress-free solution-based formula that provides savvy shortcuts and affordable, timesaving tips for overextended do-it-yourself homemakers **2:** a quick and easy equation wherein 70% ready-made convenience products are added to 30% fresh ingredients with creative personal style, allowing homemakers to take 100% of the credit for something that looks, feels, or tastes homemade **3:** a foolproof resource for having it all—and having the time to enjoy it **4:** a method created by Sandra Lee for home, garden, crafts, beauty, food, fashion, and entertaining wherein everything looks, tastes, and feels as if it was made from scratch.

Solution-based **E**nterprise that **M**otivates, **I**nspires, and **H**elps **O**rganize and **M**anage time, while **E**nriching **M**odern life by **A**dding **D**ependable shortcuts **E**very day.

TIP: Spray butter-flavor Pam® on rolling pin then dust with flour before rolling out pie crust, biscuits, or cookie dough.

dedication

Grandma always told me
Desserts are ways to show you care
My shortcuts simplify it all
So you have time to spare.

Cookies, tarts, pastries, and bars
They're easy as pie to make
You can even chill a cheesecake
If you're craving it no-bake.

When jobs, kids, and budgets
Overextend you more each day
Semi-Homemade® lets you savor
The sweet treats along the way.
XO —SL

To my sweet angel
Aspen,
Happy 15th birthday, baby.
You have filled each day with
joy, love, laughter, and fun.
xo—sl

3

Table of Contents

Chapter 1

Cakes
18

Chapter 3

Heirloom
Desserts
58

Chapter 2

Pies and Tarts
36

Chapter 4

Sandy's Sandies
102

Letter from Sandra

I've sampled desserts from all over the world, but the best ones I ever had came from my grandma's kitchen. Gateau Moelleux au Chocolat may enchant my eye and Spago's ginger crème brûlée may melt on my tongue, but it's vanilla cake with buttercream frosting that brings joy to my heart.

Some of my happiest memories are of baking with Grandma Lorraine in our little California cottage. Under her watchful eye and steady hand, desserts became works of art—towering tortes with fruit-flavored frosting, pies glistening with buttery cinnamon, fudge brownies cloaked in drifts of snowy sugar. She was a master at decoration, and her cupcakes and cookies were the first to sell at church bake sales. Friends asked her to bake cakes for their special occasions. A neighborhood wedding or birthday meant hours in the kitchen, selecting the right ingredients and thoughtfully decorating everything just so. Though her budget was small, her heart was large, and she refused to allow anyone to pay for the desserts she made. They were gifts, her way to give something that meant more than money.

I was her willing helper, though I received far more than I gave. "Be generous," she'd say, as she piped frosting or tossed candy sprinkles. "Use more sugar and less salt." "You never know till you try." As we sifted and stirred and sprinkled, I learned that kindness is measured in cupfuls, not dollars. Love isn't for sale; it's to be given freely and relished fully. And there's always room for one more—whether it's a cookie, a cupcake or a friend.

The recipe for Semi-Homemade® was concocted right there, as I watched Grandma add a pinch of this and a pat of that to boxed mixes and canned frostings to make them her own. She was always willing to experiment, eager to find a shortcut that would help her do more with less. I learned to make smart substitutions, using quality convenience products to save time and money. It evolved into my unique 70/30 philosophy: Mix 70% readymade foods with 30% fresh ingredients to bake up something that's 100% fast, fun, and fabulous! It's a formula that works for everything and everyone, from busy parents to busy professionals, especially those who are both in one!

Like my *Semi-Homemade® Desserts*, this book is a mix of old favorites and updated classics—ten luscious chapters filled with easy indulgences, from cakes, cupcakes, and cookies to pies, brownies, and bars. There are chocolate confections for those who love dessert rich, dark, and delicious and "Embellish Me" recipes for those who want to assemble and serve. Planning a party? There's something for every sweet soiree you can imagine, from the Christmas get-togethers to creative kid's birthday parties. There's even a chapter filled with sandies—crunchy, fun-filled variations on nostalgic pecan sandies. Of course, my most cherished chapter is "Heirloom Desserts"—a treasury of my family's favorite from-scratch recipes and updated, yet much quicker versions of each.

Grandma Lorraine taught me well: while success is sweet, it's best measured in the lives you touch and the friends you make. Life is a gift—and so is dessert. Let Semi-Homemade® add pleasure to both.

Cheers to a happy, healthy life!

Sandra Lee

Simple and Sweet

No time for dessert but still craving that after-dinner treat? Try an easy-as-pie cobbler, made out of refrigerated crescent roll dough and filled to the brim with your desired flavor of pie filling.

Quick-Fix Goodies

Ice Cream Sandwich Sundae:
Place a scoop of softened
strawberry ice cream between
two soft chocolate cookies. Press
the cookies together until the
ice cream comes to the edges
of the cookies. Place cookie
sandwich in a dessert bowl, top
with whipped cream, chopped
toasted pecans, chocolate sauce,
and sliced strawberries.

Drizzled Pound Cake: Make
a powdered sugar glaze by
whisking 1 cup sifted powdered
sugar with 2 tablespoons milk.
Drizzle over thawed frozen
pound cake.

Chocolate Cups with Fruit: Fill
store-bought chocolate cups
with fresh fruit and drizzle
with caramel sauce.

Mocha Pudding Cups: Perk up
chocolate or vanilla pudding with
a spoonful of flavored instant
coffee mix. Top pudding with
whipped cream.

Ice Cream Sandwich Sundae

Drizzled Pound Cake

Chocolate Cups with Fruit

Mocha Pudding Cups

Quick-Scratch Recipes
Flaky Pie Crust

Prep 15 minutes
Makes 2 (9-inch) crusts

2½	cups all-purpose flour
2	tablespoons sugar
½	teaspoon salt
1½	sticks (¾ cup) cold butter, cut into pieces
½	cup vegetable shortening, cut into small pieces, *Crisco®*
2	tablespoons (or more if necessary) ice water

1. In a large bowl, sift together flour, sugar, and salt. Add butter and shortening pieces; use your fingertips to rub butter and shortening into flour until mixture resembles fine crumbs. Add water, 1 tablespoon at a time, adding just enough to make a dough that comes together. Do not overwork. Dough should be tacky, but not sticky.

2. Roll dough into 2 balls. Flatten each ball into a disk and wrap with plastic wrap. Chill in refrigerator for at least 1 hour.

3. On a floured flat working surface, use a rolling pin to roll out 1 portion of the dough into a 12-inch circle, rotating the dough a quarter of a turn after every outward roll. Lift dough gently and transfer to a 9-inch pie plate. Press dough into pie plate and crimp edges.

4. Repeat with remaining dough to make another piecrust or use as a top crust.

5. Bake crust as directed in desired recipe or fill with desired filling and bake as directed in desired recipe.

LUSCIOUS CHOCOLATE PIE: Preheat oven to 450 degrees F. Prepare pie crust as directed. Line pie crust with double thickness of foil. Bake pie crust in preheated oven for 8 minutes. Remove foil. Bake 6 to 8 minutes more or until golden. Cool completely. Prepare two four-serving packages of chocolate pudding and pie filling (*Jell-O®*) according to package directions. Pour prepared pudding into baked pie crust. Chill in the refrigerator according to package directions. Before serving, spoon whipped dessert topping (*Cool Whip®*) over pie. Top with chocolate curls (optional).

ICE CREAM PARLOR PIE: Preheat oven to 450 degrees F. Prepare pie crust as directed. Line pie crust with double thickness of foil. Bake pie crust in preheated oven for 8 minutes. Remove foil. Bake 6 to 8 minutes more or until golden. Cool completely. Fill the pie shell with scoops of butter pecan ice cream. Drizzle with chocolate and caramel sauces. Sprinkle with chopped candy bars (optional).

Luscious Chocolate Pie

Ice Cream Parlor Pie

Quick-Scratch Recipes
Sour Cream Cake

Prep 10 minutes   **Bake** 40 minutes
Makes 9 servings

Cherry-Almond Sour Cream Cake

Strawberry-Poppy Seed Sour Cream Cake

Nonstick spray for baking, *Pam*®
1   **cup sugar**
3   **eggs**
5   **tablespoons butter, softened**
1   **teaspoon vanilla extract,** *McCormick*®
1   **cup all-purpose flour**
1   **teaspoon baking powder**
½   **cup sour cream**
    Vanilla frosting, *Betty Crocker*® **(optional)**
    Cocoa powder (optional)
    Fresh raspberries (optional)

1. Preheat oven to 325 degrees F. Spray an 8-inch square cake pan with spray for baking and set aside. In a large bowl, combine sugar, eggs, butter, and vanilla; beat with an electric mixer on medium speed about 3 minutes or until thick and lighter in color.

2. In a medium bowl, sift together flour and baking powder. Alternately add flour mixture and sour cream to egg mixture, stirring until smooth. Do not overmix. Pour into prepared pan. Bake in preheated oven for 40 to 45 minutes or until wooden pick inserted in center comes out clean. Cool on a wire rack. Frost with vanilla frosting, sprinkle with cocoa powder, and garnish with fresh raspberries (optional).

CHERRY-ALMOND SOUR CREAM CAKE: Prepare as directed, except substitute almond extract (*McCormick*®) for the vanilla extract; add ½ cup chopped dried cherries (*Sunsweet*®); and sprinkle ¼ cup sliced almonds (*Planters*®) over the batter in pan.

STRAWBERRY-POPPY SEED SOUR CREAM CAKE: Prepare as directed, except add ¼ cup poppy seed cake and pastry filling (*Solo*®), 1 teaspoon strawberry extract (*McCormick*®), and 4 drops red food coloring. Top with whipped cream and/or sugared sliced strawberries.

MAPLE-PECAN SOUR CREAM CAKE: Prepare as directed, except add ½ cup chopped candied pecans and 1 teaspoon maple flavoring (*McCormick*®).

SPICE SOUR CREAM CAKE: Prepare as directed, except substitute packed brown sugar for the sugar and add 2 tablespoons mild-flavor molasses (*Grandma's*®); 1 teaspoon pumpkin pie spice (*McCormick*®); and 1 teaspoon ground cinnamon (*McCormick*®).

TROPICAL SOUR CREAM CAKE: Prepare as directed, except substitute banana extract (*McCormick*®) for the vanilla extract and add ½ cup chopped dried pineapple and ¼ cup sweetened flaked coconut (*Baker's*®).

ESPRESSO-HAZELNUT SOUR CREAM CAKE: Prepare as directed, except add ¼ cup chocolate-hazelnut spread (*Nutella*®); ¼ cup ground hazelnuts (filberts); and 1 tablespoon espresso powder.

Quick-Scratch Recipes
Blueberry Muffins

Prep 20 minutes   Bake 26 minutes
Cool 5 minutes   Makes 12 muffins

Nonstick spray for baking, *Pam*®
2¾   **cups all-purpose flour**
¾   **cup sugar**
1   **teaspoon baking powder**
½   **teaspoon baking soda**
1   **pinch salt**
1   **cup buttermilk**
2   **eggs**
½   **cup canola oil**
1   **cup fresh blueberries**

1. Move oven rack to lowest position in oven and preheat oven to 400 degrees F. Spray twelve 2½-inch muffin cups with spray for baking and set aside. In a large bowl, sift together flour, sugar, baking powder, baking soda, and salt.

2. In a small bowl, whisk together buttermilk, eggs, and oil. Pour into flour mixture and stir together just until combined. Gently stir in blueberries. Spoon into prepared muffin cups, filling each two-thirds full. Bake in preheated oven for 26 to 30 minutes or until wooden pick inserted in centers comes out clean. Cool in pan on wire rack for 5 minutes. Remove muffins from muffin cups; cool completely on wire rack.

NUTS AND BERRIES MUFFINS: Prepare as directed, except reduce blueberries to ½ cup and add ½ cup chopped walnuts; ¼ cup sweetened dried cherries (*Sunsweet*®); and 1 teaspoon raspberry extract (*McCormick*®) with the flour.

CHOCOLATE CHIP MUFFINS: Prepare as directed, except substitute 1 cup miniature semisweet chocolate chips (*Nestlé*®) for the blueberries.

DELUXE CHOCOLATE CHIP MUFFINS: Prepare as directed, except substitute ¼ cup semisweet chocolate chips (*Nestlé*®) for the blueberries and add ¼ cup white baking chips (*Nestlé*®) and ¼ cup toffee chips (*Heath*®).

CHOCOLATE BLUEBERRY MUFFINS: Prepare as directed, except add ¼ cup unsweetened cocoa powder (*Hershey's*®) and ¼ cup sugar with the flour.

GLAZED BLUEBERRY MUFFINS: Prepare and bake muffins as directed. For glaze, in a small bowl, combine ¾ cup powdered sugar (*C&H*®); 1½ tablespoons whipping cream; and ½ teaspoon extract of your choice, stirring until a glaze consistency. Drizzle about 1 tablespoon of the glaze over each muffin.

LEMON BLUEBERRY MUFFINS: Prepare as directed, except add 2 teaspoons finely shredded lemon zest with the flour.

Nuts and Berries Muffins

Chocolate Chip Muffins

Quick-Scratch Recipes
Classic Currant Scones

Prep 25 minutes   Bake 15 minutes
Makes 12 scones

Rum-Raisin Scones

Date-Pecan Scones

2½	cups all-purpose flour
1	cup cake flour
⅔	cup sugar
1	tablespoon plus 1 teaspoon baking powder
1	pinch salt
1	stick (½ cup) cold butter, cut into pieces
1	cup buttermilk
1	egg
½	cup dried currants, *Sun-Maid*®
	Coarse sugar (optional)
	Raspberry jam, *Smucker's*® (optional)

1. Preheat oven to 425 degrees F. Line 2 baking sheets with parchment paper and set aside. In a large bowl, sift together both flours, sugar, baking powder, and salt. Add butter pieces; use your fingertips to rub butter into flour until mixture is coarse with pea-size pieces.

2. In a small bowl, whisk together buttermilk and egg. Pour into flour mixture and stir just until combined. (Do not overmix.) Gently stir in currants.

3. On a floured flat working surface, use your fingertips to press dough into a large circle, ½ inch thick. Cut into 12 wedges. Place 6 wedges on each prepared baking sheet, evenly spacing triangles. Brush with additional buttermilk and sprinkle with coarse sugar (optional).

4. Bake in preheated oven for 15 to 18 minutes or until golden brown. Serve warm or at room temperature. Serve with raspberry jam (optional).

RUM-RAISIN SCONES: Prepare as directed, except substitute ½ cup golden raisins (*Sun-Maid*®) soaked overnight in ¼ cup spiced rum (*Captain Morgan*®) for the currants (drain raisins before using). Also, add 1 teaspoon rum extract (*McCormick*®) to the batter.

DATE-PECAN SCONES: Prepare as directed, except omit currants and add ½ cup chopped pecans (*Planters*®) and ¼ cup date cake and pastry filling (*Solo*®). Serve with purchased caramel sauce.

GINGER-LEMON SCONES: Prepare as directed, except omit currants; add 1 tablespoon chopped crystallized ginger (*Reed's*®); 2 teaspoons finely shredded lemon zest; and ¼ teaspoon ground ginger (*McCormick*®).

CRANBERRY ORANGE SCONES: Prepare as directed, except substitute ½ cup sweetened dried cranberries (*Craisins*®) for the currants and add 1 teaspoon orange extract (*McCormick*®).

Cakes

1. **Two coats to perfection.** To make cakes look bakery-perfect, apply a thin layer of frosting with a long metal spatula. Let the cake set, then finish with a second, thicker coat.

2. **A light dusting.** When making a chocolate cake, dust greased pans with powdered cocoa instead of flour. It adds extra flavor and prevents white flakes.

3. **A decorator's spin.** Set your cake plate on a lazy Susan to make frosting and decorating easier.

4. **Hostess gifts.** Treat party hosts to a morning-after breakfast. Bake a coffee cake in a fluted tube pan, wrap it in cellophane, tie a ribbon around it, and present the cake in the pan as a hostess gift.

5. **Shapely cakes.** Bake cakes in shaped pans to create a fun theme. Try a football pan to celebrate the big game, a heart for Valentine's Day and birthdays or a bell to ring in the New Year and the Fourth of July.

The Recipes

Coconut Macadamia Cake

Prep 30 minutes   **Bake** 24 minutes
Makes 12 servings

COCONUT CAKE:

Nonstick spray for baking, *Pam*®

1	package (18.25-ounce) vanilla cake mix, *Betty Crocker*®
1¼	cups coconut milk, *Chaokah*®
⅓	cup vegetable oil, *Crisco*®
3	eggs

COCONUT-MACADAMIA FILLING:

½	cup evaporated milk, *Carnation*®
½	cup sugar
½	stick (¼ cup) butter
½	teaspoon vanilla extract, *McCormick*®
2	egg yolks
¾	cup shredded coconut
½	cup macadamia nuts, chopped

COCONUT ICING:

¾	cup shredded coconut
1	teaspoon rum extract, *McCormick*®
1	pinch kosher salt
2	cans (12 ounces each) whipped cream frosting, *Betty Crocker*®
½	cup shredded coconut, toasted* (optional)

1. Preheat oven to 350 degrees F. Spray two 9-inch round cake pans with nonstick spray. For Coconut Cake, in a large bowl, combine cake mix, coconut milk, oil, and eggs; beat with an electric mixer on low speed for 30 seconds. Scrape down sides of the bowl and beat on medium speed for 2 minutes more. Pour batter into prepared cake pans. Bake in preheated oven for 24 to 28 minutes or until wooden pick inserted in centers comes out clean. Cool cakes in pans on wire racks for 10 minutes. Remove cake layers from pans; cool completely on wire racks.

2. For Coconut-Macadamia Filling, in a medium saucepan, combine evaporated milk, sugar, butter, and vanilla extract. Bring to boiling, stirring constantly. In a small bowl, beat egg yolks; pour a small amount of the milk mixture into yolks. Pour back into milk mixture and continue to cook, stirring constantly, until thick. Remove from heat and stir in coconut and nuts. Cool to room temperature, then refrigerate until ready to use.

3. For Coconut Icing, in a medium bowl, stir to combine the ¾ cup shredded coconut, the rum extract, salt, and frosting. To assemble the cake, place one cake layer on a serving plate. Evenly spread Coconut-Macadamia Filling over cake layer on serving plate; top with the remaining cake layer. Frost cake with Coconut Icing. Sprinkle the ½ cup toasted coconut on top (optional).

*NOTE: To toast coconut, seeds, or nuts, place in a dry skillet over medium-low heat and stir occasionally until golden brown.

Pink Party Cake

Prep 25 minutes   **Bake** 28 minutes
Chill 20 minutes   **Makes** 10 servings

	Nonstick spray for baking, *Pam®*
1	package (18.25-ounce) strawberry cake mix, *Betty Crocker®*
1¼	cups strawberry nectar, *Kern's®*
⅓	cup vegetable oil, *Crisco®*
3	eggs
1	teaspoon almond extract, *McCormick®*
2	drops red food coloring, *McCormick®*
1	bar (4-ounce) white baking bar, chopped, *Ghirardelli®*
2	tablespoons whipping cream
1½	cans (12 ounces each) whipped fluffy white frosting, *Betty Crocker®*
1	cup pink candy coating*

1. Preheat oven to 350 degrees F. Spray two 8-inch round cake pans with nonstick spray and set aside.

2. In a large bowl, combine cake mix, strawberry nectar, oil, eggs, almond extract, and red food coloring; beat with an electric mixer on low speed for 30 seconds. Scrape down sides of the bowl and beat on medium speed for 2 minutes. Pour batter into prepared cake pans.

3. Bake in preheated oven for 28 to 32 minutes or until wooden pick inserted in centers comes out clean. Cool cakes in pans on wire racks for 10 minutes. Remove cake layers from pans; cool completely on wire racks.

4. For frosting, place chopped white baking bar in a medium bowl; set aside. In a small microwave-safe bowl, microwave cream on high setting (100 percent power) for 30 seconds. Pour over baking bar and stir until smooth. Stir in frosting. Place a cake layer on a serving plate. Spread with some of the frosting and top with the remaining cake layer. Frost cake with the remaining frosting.

5. Line a 5½-inch glass bowl with foil and set aside. Place candy coating in a small microwave-safe bowl; microwave on medium setting (50 percent power) for 1½ minutes, stirring every 30 seconds. Pour melted candy coating into foil-lined bowl and chill in refrigerator about 20 minutes or until hard.

6. Lift candy coating from bowl and peel off foil. Turn candy coating over and pull a vegetable peeler along outside edge to make large curls. Arrange pink curls on top of frosted cake.

*NOTE: Candy coating is available at cake decorating supply stores. If you can't find it, substitute the same amount of chopped vanilla bark. Melt as directed; stir in 1 to 2 drops of red food coloring to make the bark pink. Continue as directed.

Peaches and Cream Cake

Prep 25 minutes   **Bake** 35 minutes
Makes 10 servings

Nonstick spray for baking, *Pam®*
1   **package (18.25-ounce) vanilla cake mix, *Betty Crocker®***
1   **cup sour cream**
¾   **cup cake flour, *Swans Down®***
1   **cup peach nectar, *Kern's®***
⅓   **cup vegetable oil, *Crisco®***
4   **eggs**
8   **drops red food coloring, *McCormick®***
4   **drops yellow food coloring, *McCormick®***
1½   **cups frozen unsweetened peach slices, finely chopped, *Dole®***
2   **cans (12 ounces each) whipped buttercream frosting, *Betty Crocker®***

1. Preheat oven to 350 degrees F. Spray two 9-inch round cake pans with nonstick spray. In a large bowl, combine cake mix, sour cream, cake flour, peach nectar, oil, eggs, and food colorings; beat with an electric mixer on low speed for 30 seconds. Scrape sides of the bowl; beat on medium speed for 2 minutes more. Stir in the 1½ cups peaches. Pour batter into prepared pans. Bake for 35 to 40 minutes or until wooden pick inserted comes out clean. Cool cakes in pans for 10 minutes. Remove cake from pans; cool completely. Place a cake layer on a serving plate. Spread with ¾ cup of the buttercream frosting; top with the remaining cake layer. Frost cake. Garnish with additional thawed, drained *peach slices* (optional).

Apple Upside-Down Cake

Prep 30 minutes   **Bake** 50 minutes
Cool 30 minutes   **Makes** 12 servings

Nonstick spray for baking, *Pam®*
1½   **cups caramel topping, *Smucker's®***
2   **cans (21 ounces each) apple pie filling, *Comstock® More Fruit***
1   **package (18.25-ounce) butter recipe yellow cake mix, *Betty Crocker®***
1   **cup water**
1   **stick (½ cup) butter, softened**
3   **eggs**
½   **cup unsweetened applesauce, *Mott's®***
3   **packets (0.74 ounce each) spiced cider drink mix, *Alpine®***

1. Preheat oven to 350 degrees F. Spray the sides of two 9-inch round cake pans with nonstick spray. Pour ¾ cup of the caramel topping into each cake pan; spread evenly. Arrange apple slices from 1 can of the pie filling in a decorative pattern on top of the caramel topping in 1 pan. Repeat with the remaining can of pie filling and the other cake pan. Carefully spoon the remainder of the pie filling over the apple slices.

2. In a large bowl, combine cake mix, the water, butter, eggs, applesauce, and cider drink mix; beat with an electric mixer on low speed for 30 seconds. Scrape down sides of the bowl and beat on medium speed for 2 minutes more. Gently pour half of the batter over apple slices in each cake pan. Bake for 50 to 55 minutes or until wooden pick inserted in centers comes out clean. Cool cakes in pans on wire racks for 30 minutes. Turn each cake pan over onto a rimmed serving plate; gently lift pans to remove cakes. Serve immediately.

Dulce de Leche Cake

Prep 15 minutes   **Bake** 30 minutes
Makes 12 servings

Nonstick vegetable cooking spray, *Pam®*
1   package (18.25-ounce) butter recipe yellow cake mix, *Betty Crocker®*
2½   cups dulce de leche ice cream, melted, *Häagen-Dazs®*
3   eggs
1   package (8-ounce) cream cheese, softened, *Philadelphia®*
¼   cup caramel topping, *Smucker's®*

1. Preheat oven to 350 degrees F. Spray a 9-inch tube cake pan with cooking spray and set aside. In a large bowl, combine cake mix, 2 cups of the melted ice cream, and the eggs; beat with an electric mixer on low speed for 30 seconds. Using a rubber spatula, scrape down sides of the bowl and beat on medium speed about 2 minutes more or until thickened. Pour into prepared cake pan.

2. Bake in preheated oven for 30 to 35 minutes or until wooden pick inserted in center comes out clean. Cool cake in pan on a wire rack. In a large bowl, combine cream cheese, caramel topping, and the remaining ½ cup melted ice cream; beat with an electric mixer on low speed until smooth. Turn cooled cake over on a serving plate; gently lift pan to remove cake. Cut cake into slices. Spoon cream cheese mixture over cake slices.

Lemon-Poppy Seed Cake

Prep 20 minutes   **Bake** 40 minutes
Makes 10 servings

Nonstick spray for baking, *Pam®*
1   large lemon
1   package (18.25-ounce) yellow cake mix, *Betty Crocker®*
1   cup buttermilk
⅓   cup vegetable oil, *Crisco®*
3   eggs
½   cup poppy seed cake and pastry filling, *Solo®*
2   cups powdered sugar, sifted, *C&H®*
2   tablespoons buttermilk
3   tablespoons lemon juice (reserved from lemon above)
2   drops yellow food coloring, *McCormick®*

1. For cake, preheat oven to 350 degrees F. Spray a tall 9-inch fluted tube cake pan with nonstick spray. Finely shred zest from lemon; squeeze juice from lemon. In a large bowl, combine cake mix, buttermilk, oil, eggs, all of the finely shredded lemon zest, and 3 tablespoons of the lemon juice; beat with an electric mixer on low speed for 30 seconds. Scrape down sides of the bowl and beat on medium speed for 2 minutes more. Stir in poppy seed filling until well mixed. Pour batter into prepared pan. Bake in preheated oven for 40 to 45 minutes or until wooden pick inserted in center of the cake comes out clean. Cool cake in pan on wire rack. Turn cooled cake over on a serving plate; gently lift pan to remove cake.

2. For glaze, stir together powdered sugar, buttermilk, lemon juice, and yellow food coloring until a smooth, glaze consistency. Drizzle glaze over top and down sides of cake. Serve with *halved strawberries* (optional).

Raspberry Ripple Cake

Prep 25 minutes   **Bake** 38 minutes
Makes 12 servings

RASPBERRY RIPPLE CAKE:
Nonstick spray for baking, *Pam*®
1   package (18.25-ounce) white cake mix, *Betty Crocker*®
1¼   cups white cranberry juice, *Ocean Spray*®
⅓   cup vegetable oil, *Crisco*®
3   egg whites
6   tablespoons red raspberry preserves, *Smucker's*®
¼   teaspoon raspberry extract, *McCormick*®
⅛   teaspoon red food coloring, *McCormick*®

VANILLA ICING:
1   cup powdered sugar, sifted, *C&H*®
5   tablespoons whipping cream
1   teaspoon vanilla extract, *McCormick*®

RASPBERRY GLAZE:
¼   cup red raspberry preserves, *Smucker's*®
1½   teaspoons white cranberry juice, *Ocean Spray*®

1. For Raspberry Ripple Cake, preheat oven to 350 degrees F. Spray a 9-inch fluted tube pan with nonstick spray and set aside.

2. In a large bowl, combine cake mix, white cranberry juice, oil, and egg whites; beat with an electric mixer on low speed for 30 seconds. Using a rubber spatula, scrape down sides of the bowl and beat on medium speed for 2 minutes more. Transfer 1 cup of the batter to a small bowl; stir in raspberry preserves, raspberry extract, and red food coloring. Pour half of the white cake batter into prepared pan. Top with raspberry cake batter. Top with the remaining white cake batter.

3. Bake in preheated oven for 38 to 40 minutes or until wooden pick inserted in center of cake comes out clean. Cool cake in pan on a wire rack.

4. For Vanilla Icing, in a small bowl, combine powdered sugar, whipping cream, and vanilla; beat with electric mixer on medium speed until a smooth, thin consistency.

5. For Raspberry Glaze, in a small bowl, thoroughly combine raspberry preserves and cranberry juice. Turn cooled cake over onto a serving plate and gently lift pan to remove cake. Spread Vanilla Icing over top and down sides of cake. Drizzle with Raspberry Glaze.

Orange-Vanilla Cake

Prep 25 minutes   **Bake** 40 minutes
Makes 12 servings

Nonstick spray for baking, *Pam®*
1   orange
1   vanilla bean
1   **package (18.25-ounce) butter recipe yellow cake mix,** *Betty Crocker®*
¾   **cup orange marmalade,** *Knott's®*
1   **stick (½ cup) butter, softened**
3   **eggs**
1   **can (12-ounce) whipped buttercream frosting,** *Betty Crocker®*
½   **teaspoon orange extract,** *McCormick®*
1   **pinch kosher salt**
     Orange peel shreds (optional)

1. Preheat oven to 350 degrees F. Spray a 9-inch tube cake pan with nonstick spray and set aside.

2. Finely shred zest from orange; squeeze juice from orange. Add enough water to orange juice to make 1¼ cups total liquid. Using a sharp knife, cut vanilla bean in half lengthwise; use tip of knife to scrape seeds from the inside of the vanilla bean. Set aside.

3. In a large bowl, combine cake mix, orange juice-water mixture, ¼ cup of the marmalade, the butter, eggs, and half of the scraped vanilla bean seeds; beat with an electric mixer on low speed for 30 seconds. Using rubber spatula, scrape down sides of the bowl and beat on medium speed for 2 minutes. Pour batter into prepared cake pan. Bake in preheated oven for 40 to 45 minutes or until wooden pick inserted in center of the cake comes out clean. Cool cake in pan on a wire rack.

4. In a medium bowl, stir together buttercream frosting, 1 tablespoon of the orange zest, the orange extract, salt, and the remaining scraped vanilla bean seeds; cover and set aside.

5. Turn cooled cake over on a wire rack and gently lift pan to remove cake. Cut cake in half horizontally and place bottom half on a serving plate. Spread with the remaining ½ cup marmalade and place the remaining cake on top. Frost cake with buttercream icing. Garnish with orange peel shreds (optional).

Pineapple Poke Cake

Nonstick spray for baking, *Pam*®
1   package (18.25-ounce) butter recipe yellow cake mix, *Betty Crocker*®
1   package (4-serving-size) instant lemon pudding and pie filling, *Jell-O*®
1¼ cups pineapple juice, *Dole*®
1   stick (½ cup) butter, softened
3   eggs
1½ cups sour cream
1   cup powdered sugar, sifted, *C&H*®
1¼ cups pineapple soda, *Fanta*®

1. Preheat oven to 350 degrees F. Spray a fluted tube cake pan with nonstick spray. In a bowl, combine cake mix and 3 tablespoons of the dry instant pudding. Add pineapple juice, butter, and eggs; beat with an electric mixer on low speed for 30 seconds. Scrape bowl; beat on medium speed for 2 minutes more. Pour batter into prepared pan. Bake for 40 to 45 minutes or until wooden pick inserted comes out clean. Cool in pan.

2. For icing, combine sour cream and the remaining dry instant pudding; beat with an electric mixer on low speed until smooth. Gradually add powdered sugar; beat until smooth. Remove cake from pan; place on plate. Using a skewer, poke holes in the cake top. Slowly pour pineapple soda over holes. Spread icing over cake. Garnish with *lemon peel curls.*

Confetti Cake

Nonstick spray for baking, *Pam*®
1   package (18.25-ounce) white cake mix, *Betty Crocker*®
1¼ cups pear nectar, *Kern's*®
½   cup plus 1 tablespoon liquid egg whites, *All Whites*®
⅓   cup vegetable oil, *Crisco*®
1   teaspoon strawberry extract, *McCormick*®
2   bottles (1.25 ounces each) colored snowflake sprinkles, *Cake Mate*®
2   cups powdered sugar, sifted, *C&H*®
5   tablespoons strawberry milk, *Nesquik*®
1   teaspoon strawberry extract, *McCormick*®

1. For cake, preheat oven to 350 degrees F. Spray a fluted tube cake pan with nonstick spray. In a bowl, combine cake mix, pear nectar, egg whites, oil, and strawberry extract; beat with an electric mixer on low speed for 30 seconds. Using a rubber spatula, scrape down sides of the bowl and beat on medium speed for 2 minutes more. Reserve 1 tablespoon sprinkles; stir in remaining sprinkles. Pour batter into prepared pan. Bake in preheated oven for 45 to 50 minutes or until wooden pick inserted in center of the cake comes out clean. Cool cake in pan on wire rack.

2. For glaze, in a small bowl, stir together powdered sugar, strawberry milk, and strawberry extract until a glaze consistency. Turn cooled cake over onto a serving plate and gently lift pan to remove cake. Drizzle glaze over cake; immediately sprinkle with reserved sprinkles.

Red Velvet Pound Cake

Prep 20 minutes   **Bake** 65 minutes
Makes 8 servings

Nonstick spray for baking, *Pam*®
¾   cup low-fat chocolate milk, *Nesquik*®
1   tablespoon red food coloring, *McCormick*®
1   package (16-ounce) pound cake mix, *Betty Crocker*®
¼   cup unsweetened cocoa powder, *Hershey's*®
2   eggs
1   package (12-ounce) miniature chocolate chips, *Nestlé*®
1   can (12-ounce) whipped cream cheese frosting, *Betty Crocker*®

1. Preheat oven to 350 degrees F. Spray a 9×5-inch loaf pan with nonstick spray. In a liquid measuring cup, combine chocolate milk and food coloring.

2. In a large bowl, combine cake mix, cocoa powder, and eggs; beat with an electric mixer on low speed for 30 seconds. Add chocolate milk mixture and beat on medium speed for 3 minutes more, scraping down sides of bowl frequently. Stir in chocolate chips. Pour batter into prepared loaf pan. Bake in preheated oven for 65 to 75 minutes or until wooden pick inserted in center comes out clean. Cool cake in pan on a wire rack.

3. Remove cake from pan and rub sides to loosen any crumbs, collecting crumbs and setting them aside. Frost cake with cream cheese frosting. Sprinkle reserved cake crumbs on cake.

Peanut Butter Cake

Prep 20 minutes   **Bake** 55 minutes
Makes 8 servings

Nonstick spray for baking, *Pam*®
1   package (16-ounce) pound cake mix, *Betty Crocker*®
¾   cup banana syrup, *Margie's*®
¼   cup crème de banana, *DeKuyper*® (or 2 teaspoons banana extract)
2   eggs
1   package (10-ounce) peanut butter chips, *Reese's*®
½   cup dried banana pieces, crushed
2   tablespoons butter
2   tablespoons whipping cream
⅓   cup chopped honey-roasted peanuts (optional)

1. Preheat oven to 350 degrees F. Spray a 9×5-inch loaf pan with nonstick spray. In a large bowl, combine cake mix, syrup, crème de banana, and eggs; beat with an electric mixer on low speed for 30 seconds. Scrape bowl; beat on medium speed for 3 minutes more. Stir in 1 cup of the peanut butter chips and the crushed dried banana. Pour batter into prepared pan. Bake in preheated oven for 55 to 60 minutes or until a wooden pick inserted comes out clean. Cool cake in pan on a wire rack.

2. For glaze, in a small microwave-safe bowl, combine the remaining peanut butter chips, the butter, and whipping cream; microwave on medium setting (50 percent power) for 1½ minutes, stirring every 30 seconds. Remove cake from pan and pour glaze over top. Garnish with chopped honey-roasted peanuts (optional).

Pies and Tarts

1. **Fix-up frozen.** Stock a few frozen pies and you'll always be ready for guests. Garnish pies to echo the ingredients inside. Fan cinnamon-sprinkled apple slices on top of apple pie, use sugared lime wedges for key lime, or white and dark chocolate curls for chocolate.

2. **Pretty piping.** For a prettier presentation, pipe stiff whipped cream through a star or rosette decorating tip.

3. **Spice it up.** Flavor warm dessert sauces with fragrant spices, such as cinnamon, cloves, ginger, cardamom, mace, or nutmeg.

4. **Clean slices.** Dip your knife in cold water to keep it from sticking to the meringue when you slice a pie.

5. **Easy pumpkin pie.** For an easy pumpkin mousse, combine a can of pumpkin pie filling with a container of Cool Whip®. Serve in a wine goblet, topped with crumbled graham crackers, a sprinkling of pumpkin pie spice, and a cinnamon stick garnish.

The Recipes

Washington Cherry Pie

Prep 30 minutes   Bake 35 minutes
Makes 8 servings

1	package (15-ounce) refrigerated rolled piecrust (2 crusts), *Pillsbury®*
1	can (21-ounce) red cherry pie filling, *Comstock® More Fruit*
2	cups frozen dark sweet cherries, thawed, cut in half, *Dole®*
¼	cup granulated sugar
1	tablespoon quick-cooking tapioca, *Minute®*
¼	teaspoon ground nutmeg, *McCormick®*
1	tablespoon cold butter, cut into pieces
¼	teaspoon cherry extract, *McCormick®*
1	egg, lightly beaten
2	tablespoons sparkling sugar

1. Preheat oven to 425 degrees F. Line a baking sheet with foil. Unroll one of the piecrusts on the back of another lightly floured baking sheet and cut into ten to twelve 1-inch-wide strips. Remove every other strip and lay it horizontally over the dough strips on the foil. For a lattice, weave each strip over and under the other strips, starting with middle horizontal strip. Place latticed dough in the refrigerator until ready to use.

2. Unroll the remaining piecrust and press onto bottom and sides of a 9-inch pie plate; set aside.

3. In a large bowl, combine pie filling, thawed cherries, granulated sugar, tapioca, and nutmeg; stir until well mixed. Pour cherry mixture into crust and dot with butter pieces.

4. Add cherry extract to beaten egg and mix to make an egg wash. Using a pastry brush, brush egg wash over edge of the crust. Remove latticed dough from refrigerator and carefully slide over cherry mixture. If necessary, carefully adjust any strips. Crimp crust edges together. Brush egg wash on strips and sprinkle with sparkling sugar. Place pie on foil-lined baking sheet.

5. Bake in preheated oven for 35 to 40 minutes or until crust is golden brown and fruit is bubbling. (Cover edge of pie with foil if it begins to brown too quickly.) Cool completely on a wire rack.

38 | Pies and Tarts

S'More Pie

Prep 10 minutes   **Bake** 40 minutes
Makes 2 pies (8 servings each)

1	package (18.3-ounce) fudge brownie mix, *Betty Crocker®*
⅔	cup vegetable oil, *Crisco®*
¼	cup water
2	eggs
3	cups miniature marshmallows, *Jet-Puffed®*
1	cup whole almonds, chopped, *Planters®*
2	(9-inch) shortbread crusts, *Keebler® Ready Crust®*
1½	cups miniature marshmallows, *Jet-Puffed®*

1. Preheat oven to 350 degrees F. In a large bowl, combine brownie mix, oil, water, and eggs; stir with a wooden spoon until well mixed. Stir in the 3 cups marshmallows and almonds.

2. Divide batter between shortbread crusts, filling each three-fourths full. Bake in preheated oven for 35 to 40 minutes. Divide remaining miniature marshmallows between pies, sprinkling evenly over tops of pies. Bake for 5 minutes more or just until set in center. Cool completely on wire racks.

Lemon Meringue No-Bake Pie

Prep 15 minutes   **Chill** 4 hours
Makes 8 servings

1½	cups meringue cookies
3	containers (6 ounces each) lemon yogurt, *Yoplait®*
1	package (4-serving-size) instant lemon pudding and pie filling, *Jell-O®*
1	(9-inch) shortbread crumb crust, *Keebler® Ready Crust®*
1	teaspoon lemon extract, *McCormick®*
1	container (8-ounce) frozen whipped topping, thawed, *Cool Whip®*

1. Place meringue cookies in a large zip-top bag. Press out air and seal. Using a rolling pin, roll over meringue cookies until crushed; set aside.

2. In a large bowl, combine yogurt and instant dry pudding; whisk until well mixed. Spoon into shortbread crust.

3. Stir lemon extract into whipped topping. Spoon over yogurt mixture. Sprinkle crushed meringue cookies over whipped topping. Chill in refrigerator for at least 4 hours before serving.

Banana Marshmallow Pie

Prep 30 minutes   **Bake** 15 minutes
Chill 5 hours   **Makes** 8 servings

1	refrigerated rolled piecrust (½ of a 15-ounce package), *Pillsbury®*
3	cups milk
1	package (4-serving-size) cook-and-serve banana cream pudding and pie filling, *Jell-O®*
2	jars (7 ounces each) marshmallow creme, *Jet-Puffed®*
2	large ripe bananas, sliced
1	tablespoon butter
1	cup whipping cream
	Banana slices (optional)

1. Preheat oven to 450 degrees F. Unroll piecrust and press onto bottom and sides of a 9-inch pie plate. Crimp crust edge. Using a fork, prick bottom and sides of crust. Bake in preheated oven for 15 to 17 minutes or until golden brown. Remove and cool completely.

2. In a medium saucepan, combine milk and dry banana pudding; cook and stir over medium heat until boiling. Remove from heat. Add 1 jar of the marshmallow creme, stirring until well mixed. Cool for 5 minutes.

3. Arrange banana slices in bottom of cooled crust. Pour pudding-marshmallow mixture into crust. Refrigerate about 3 hours or until set.

4. In a medium microwave-safe bowl, combine the remaining jar of marshmallow creme and the butter; microwave on high setting (100 percent power) for 1 minute, stirring every 20 seconds.

5. In a large bowl, beat whipping cream with an electric mixer on medium-high speed until soft peaks form. Gently fold melted marshmallow-butter mixture into whipped cream. Spoon onto pie. Refrigerate at least 2 hours or until ready to serve. Garnish with banana slices (optional).

Coffee Buttercrunch Pie

Prep 25 minutes   Bake 25 minutes
Chill 2 hours   Makes 8 servings

	Nonstick vegetable cooking spray, *Pam®*
1 ⅓	cups piecrust mix, *Betty Crocker®*
1	cup walnuts
⅓	cup miniature semisweet chocolate chips, *Nestlé®*
¼	cup packed brown sugar, *C&H®*
1	tablespoon plus 1 teaspoon water
2	teaspoons imitation butter flavoring, *McCormick®*
2 ¼	cups milk
1	package (4-serving-size) instant vanilla pudding and pie filling, *Jell-O®*
5	tablespoons Café Vienna coffee drink mix, *General Foods®*
2	cups frozen whipped topping, thawed, *Cool Whip®*

1. Preheat oven to 350 degrees F. Spray a 9-inch pie plate with cooking spray.

2. In a food processor, combine piecrust mix, walnuts, chocolate chips, and brown sugar. Cover and pulse just until mixture is combined. Stir together the water and 1 teaspoon of the butter flavoring; pour into crust mixture. Cover and pulse until mixture appears moist, but still crumbly. Press onto bottom and up sides of pie plate.

3. Bake in preheated oven for 25 to 30 minutes or until crust is firm and lightly browned. Cool completely on a wire rack.

4. In a large bowl, combine milk, instant dry pudding, 3 tablespoons of the coffee drink mix, and the remaining 1 teaspoon butter flavoring; whisk for 2 minutes, then let sit about 3 minutes or until thick.

5. In a medium bowl, gently stir the remaining 2 tablespoons coffee drink mix into the whipped topping. Pour pudding mixture into cooled crust. Top with whipped topping mixture. Chill in refrigerator about 2 hours or until set.

Double PB&J Pie

Prep 20 minutes   **Bake** 45 minutes
Makes 8 servings

1	pouch (17.5-ounce) peanut butter cookie mix, *Betty Crocker®*
1	stick (½ cup) butter, melted
¾	cup dark-color corn syrup, *Karo®*
½	cup creamy peanut butter, *Skippy® Natural*
3	eggs
¼	cup sugar
¼	cup strawberry jelly, *Smucker's®*
1	pint fresh strawberries, hulled and halved

1. Preheat oven to 350 degrees F. In a medium bowl, stir together cookie mix and melted butter until mixture comes together. Press into bottom and up sides of a 9-inch pie plate.

2. In a large bowl, combine corn syrup and peanut butter; beat with an electric mixer on medium speed until smooth. Add eggs and sugar; beat until smooth. Pour mixture into cookie crust.

3. Bake for 45 to 50 minutes or until set. Remove from oven; cool completely. Spread strawberry jelly in center of cooled pie. Arrange strawberry halves around jelly.

Spumoni Pie

Prep 25 minutes   **Chill** 4 hours
Makes 8 servings

¾	cup dark chocolate chips, *Nestlé® Chocolatier*
1	(9-inch) chocolate crumb crust, *Keebler® Ready Crust®*
1⅓	cups milk
1	package (4-serving-size) instant pistachio pudding and pie filling, *Jell-O®*
⅓	cup dried apricots, chopped, *Sun-Maid®*
⅓	cup dried cranberries, chopped, *Craisins®*
1½	cups frozen whipped topping, thawed, *Cool Whip® Extra Creamy*
¼	cup pistachios, chopped (optional)

1. In a small microwave-safe bowl, microwave chocolate chips on medium setting (50 percent power) for 1½ minutes, stirring every 30 seconds. Pour ⅓ cup of the chocolate into the bottom of the crust.

2. In a large bowl, combine milk and instant dry pudding; whisk for 2 minutes, then let sit about 3 minutes or until thick. Spoon pudding mixture over chocolate. Sprinkle chopped apricots and cranberries over top. Spoon whipped topping over chopped fruit.

3. Drizzle the remaining melted chocolate on top of the whipped topping in desired pattern (if chocolate has hardened, microwave for 30 seconds). If desired, garnish with chopped pistachios. Chill in refrigerator for at least 4 hours before serving.

Maple Pecan Tart

Prep 20 minutes   Bake 48 minutes
Makes 8 servings

1	refrigerated rolled piecrust (½ of a 15-ounce package), *Pillsbury*®
3	eggs
2	tablespoons sugar
¾	cup real maple syrup
1	tablespoon maple flavoring, *McCormick*®
1	teaspoon vanilla, *McCormick*®
3	tablespoons all-purpose flour
2	tablespoons butter, melted
⅛	teaspoon salt
1½	cups whole pecans, *Planters*®

1. Preheat oven to 450 degrees F. Unroll piecrust and press onto bottom and sides of a 9-inch tart pan with a removable bottom, leaving a 1-inch overhang of crust. Fold overhang inward and use your fingers to press crust into sides of tart pan. Using a fork, prick bottom and side of the crust.

2. Bake in preheated oven for 8 to 10 minutes or until lightly browned. Cool completely on a wire rack. Reduce oven temperature to 325 degrees F.

3. In a large bowl, combine eggs and sugar; beat with electric mixer on medium speed about 2 minutes or until foamy. Add maple syrup, maple flavoring, and vanilla; beat until combined. Add flour, melted butter, and salt; beat until combined.

4. Spread nuts in bottom of the cooled piecrust. Pour maple syrup mixture over nuts. Bake in preheated oven for 40 to 45 minutes or just until center is set. Cool on a wire rack. Serve warm or at room temperature.

NOTE: For a special touch, stir 1 to 2 teaspoons maple flavoring (*McCormick*®) into 1 container (8-ounce) frozen whipped topping, thawed, (*Cool Whip*®). Serve with pie.

Strawberry Poppy
Seed Tart

Prep 30 minutes   **Bake** 20 minutes
Makes 6 servings

1	pound fresh strawberries, hulled and sliced
⅓	cup poppy seed cake and pastry filling, *Solo*®
½	cup tub-style cream cheese, softened, *Philadelphia*®
¼	cup whipping cream
3	tablespoons granulated sugar
½	teaspoon vanilla extract, *McCormick*®
1	egg, lightly beaten
1	teaspoon water
1	sheet frozen puff pastry, thawed, *Pepperidge Farm*®
	Powdered sugar

1. Preheat oven to 400 degrees F. Line a baking sheet with parchment paper. In a small bowl, combine strawberries and poppy seed filling.

2. In a medium bowl, beat cream cheese with electric mixer on medium speed until fluffy. Add whipping cream and beat until soft peaks form. Beat in granulated sugar and vanilla. Refrigerate until ready to use.

3. Stir together egg and water; set aside. Unroll puff pastry sheet onto a lightly floured surface. Using a rolling pin, roll each side of the pastry sheet ¼ inch longer than original. Using a sharp knife, cut a ¾-inch-wide strip from each side of the pastry dough. Using a pastry brush, brush egg mixture around edges of dough rectangle. To make a raised edge for tart, place each dough strip on top of the side it was cut from and trim off excess dough. Using a fork, prick bottom of the tart dough. Brush egg mixture over top edge. Bake in preheated oven for 20 to 25 minutes or until puffed and golden brown. Cool completely on a wire rack.

4. Fill cooled tart shell with the cream cheese mixture. Spoon strawberry-poppy seed mixture over. Dust with sifted powdered sugar and serve immediately.

Rhubarb Tartlets with Lemon Cream

Prep 30 minutes **Bake** 20 minutes
Stand 45 minutes **Makes** 4 tartlets

1	sheet frozen puff pastry, thawed, *Pepperidge Farm*®
1	egg, lightly beaten
1	teaspoon water
1	package (16-ounce) frozen rhubarb, thawed, *Dole*®
¼	cup plus 2 tablespoons lemon curd, *Dickinson's*®
¼	cup sugar
2	tablespoons crystallized ginger, finely chopped, *Reed's*®
1	tablespoon cornstarch
½	teaspoon ground ginger, *McCormick*®
⅓	cup sour cream
¼	cup frozen whipped topping, thawed, *Cool Whip*®

1. Preheat oven to 400 degrees F. Unroll puff pastry sheet onto a lightly floured surface. Using a rolling pin, roll out to a 10-inch square. Cut pastry into four 5-inch squares and press each pastry square into a 4-inch tart pan. Cut off any overhang. Using a fork, prick the bottom of the pastry in each tart pan. Stir together egg and the water; using a pastry brush, brush over each tart.

2. Bake in preheated oven for 20 to 25 minutes or until puffed and golden brown. Cool on wire rack.

3. In a medium saucepan, combine rhubarb, ¼ cup of the lemon curd, the sugar, crystallized ginger, cornstarch, and ground ginger. Cook over medium-high heat about 5 minutes or until rhubarb is soft and mixture has thickened, stirring occasionally. Remove from heat. Let stand at room temperature about 45 minutes or until cool.

4. For lemon cream, combine sour cream and the remaining 2 tablespoons lemon curd, stirring until smooth. Gently stir in whipped topping. Refrigerate until ready to use.

5. To serve, cut a circle in the middle of each puff pastry tart and gently press down middle. Spoon 6 tablespoons of the rhubarb mixture into the middle of each tart. Top each with 3 tablespoons of the lemon cream. Serve immediately.

Orange Truffle Tartlets

Prep 25 minutes   **Bake** 14 minutes
Chill 2 hours   **Makes** 4 tartlets

1	package (5.52-ounce) plain biscotti, *Nonni's®*
½	stick (¼ cup) butter, melted
1	package (10-ounce) dark chocolate chips, *Nestlé® Chocolatier*
1	cup whipping cream
½	cup orange marmalade, *Smucker's® Simply Fruit®*
2	tablespoons orange juice concentrate, *Minute Maid®*

1. Preheat oven to 350 degrees F. Break up biscotti and place in a food processor; cover and pulse until fine crumbs form. Add butter and pulse until mixture comes together. Press crumbs into bottom of four 4½-inch tart pans with removable bottoms.

2. Bake in preheated oven for 14 to 16 minutes or until golden brown. Cool completely on wire racks.

3. Place chocolate chips in a medium bowl and set aside. In a small saucepan, combine whipping cream, orange marmalade, and orange juice concentrate; cook and stir over medium heat just until boiling. Pour over chocolate chips; using a rubber spatula, stir until completely smooth.

4. Pour orange-chocolate mixture into cooled biscotti crusts.* Chill in refrigerator about 2 hours or until set.

*TIP: If any extra chocolate truffle filling remains after filling the tarts, you can serve it as a sauce over ice cream and/or fresh berries. Heat the remaining filling in the microwave on medium setting (50 percent power) for 30 seconds or until smooth and melted. Cover leftovers and store in the refrigerator for up to 3 days.

Fig and Port Tartlets

Prep 35 minutes   **Bake** 15 minutes
Makes 24 tartlets

	Nonstick vegetable cooking spray, *Pam*®
1	package (15-ounce) refrigerated rolled piecrust (2 crusts), *Pillsbury*®
2	jars (10 ounces each) fig royale preserves, *St. Dalfour*®
¼	cup port, *Fairbanks*®
½	cup whipping cream
2	tablespoons granulated sugar
½	teaspoon ground cinnamon, *McCormick*®

1. Preheat oven to 425 degrees F. Spray twenty-four 1¾-inch muffin cups with cooking spray.

2. Unroll piecrusts one at a time. Using a 2½-inch round cutter, cut as many rounds as possible (about 12); reserve scraps. Repeat with second piecrust. Gather scraps together and roll out. Cut out as many rounds as needed to make 24 rounds total. Fit dough rounds into prepared muffin cups. Using a fork, prick bottoms and sides of the tart crusts.

3. Place both muffin pans in preheated oven. Bake for 15 to 18 minutes or until golden brown. Cool completely on a wire rack.

4. In a small saucepan, stir together preserves and port. Cook and stir over medium heat about 6 minutes or until thick. Remove from heat and set aside.

5. In a large bowl, beat cream with an electric mixer on low to medium speed until soft peaks form. Add granulated sugar and cinnamon and beat just until stiff peaks form.

6. To serve, fill each tartlet with 1 tablespoon of the fig mixture and top with 2 teaspoons of the whipped cream.

Heirloom Desserts

1. **Spruce-up tradition.** Update an old recipe with new fruits. Sliced pears, figs, mangos, apricots, and rhubarb make a cake, cobbler, or pie instantly trendy.

2. **Spunky topping.** To make an old-fashioned sour cream topping, stir 6 tablespoons of lemon curd into 1 cup of sour cream. For a sweeter version, use 3 tablespoons of sugar and a teaspoon of vanilla in place of the lemon curd.

3. **Candy bar sauce.** Melt candy bars in the microwave to make a quick chocolate sauce. Hershey® bars, peppermint patties, and Snickers® bars are delicious ladled over cheesecake, ice cream, or pound cake.

4. **Vanilla sugar.** Store a vanilla bean in your sugar canister to give sugar a subtle flavor.

5. **Elegant cobbler.** Serve fruit cobbler in a wine goblet to dress up the presentation. Break the crust with a spoon so the ice cream can swirl through the fruit and top with a swizzle of jarred cabernet sauce.

The Recipes

Lattice Peach Cobbler

Prep 40 minutes   **Bake** 45 minutes
Makes 6 servings

QUICK-SCRATCH

7	cups sliced, peeled fresh peaches or frozen peaches, thawed
¾	cup plus 2 tablespoons sugar
2	tablespoons quick-cooking tapioca, *Minute*®
1	tablespoon lemon juice, *Minute Maid*®
½	teaspoon salt
5	tablespoons cold butter, cut into small pieces
1	cup all-purpose flour
1½	teaspoons baking powder
½	teaspoon ground cinnamon, *McCormick*®
6	tablespoons buttermilk
1	egg, lightly beaten
1	teaspoon water

1. Preheat oven to 400 degrees F. Grease and flour an 8-inch square baking pan.

2. In a large bowl, combine peaches, ¾ cup of the sugar, the tapioca, lemon juice, and ¼ teaspoon of the salt. Pour into prepared pan; dot with 2 tablespoons of the butter pieces.

3. In a medium bowl, sift together flour, the remaining 2 tablespoons sugar, the baking powder, cinnamon, and the remaining ¼ teaspoon salt. Add the remaining 3 tablespoons butter pieces and rub in with your fingers until mixture forms fine crumbs. Add buttermilk and mix until dough comes together.

4. On a floured surface, roll out dough into an 8-inch square; using a sharp knife, cut into 1-inch-wide strips. Place half of the strips on top of peach mixture, spacing 1 inch apart; arrange remaining strips perpendicular to first strips, weaving each strip over and under the other strips to make a lattice pattern.

5. In a small bowl, whisk together egg and the water to make an egg wash. Brush egg wash on latticed dough.

6. Bake in preheated oven for 45 to 55 minutes or until crust is golden brown and fruit is bubbling. Serve warm

Santa Fe Fruit Cobbler

Prep 20 minutes   **Bake** 50 minutes
Makes 10 servings

	Nonstick vegetable cooking spray, *Pam®*
1	**can (21-ounce) raspberry pie filling**, *Comstock® More Fruit* or *Wilderness® More Fruit*
1	**package (16-ounce) frozen mango chunks, thawed**, *Dole®*
1	**can (15-ounce) apricot halves, drained, cut in half**, *Del Monte®*
½	**cup apricot preserves**, *Knott's®*
⅓	**cup sugar**
1	**can (11-ounce) mexicorn, drained**, *Green Giant®*
½	**cup sour cream**
1	**package (14-ounce) honey corn bread mix**, *Krusteaz®*
¼	**cup diced green chiles**, *Ortega®*
2	**tablespoons butter, melted**

1. Preheat oven to 350 degrees F. Spray a 9×13-inch glass baking dish with cooking spray.

2. In a large bowl, stir together raspberry pie filling, mango, apricots, apricot preserves, and sugar. Spoon into prepared pan; set aside.

3. In a food processor, combine mexicorn and sour cream; cover and process until smooth. Transfer to a large bowl. Add corn bread mix, green chiles, and melted butter; stir until well mixed. Using a large ice cream scoop, scoop batter over fruit mixture, spacing evenly.

4. Bake in preheated oven for 50 to 60 minutes or until bubbling and corn bread is baked through. Serve warm.

Peach and Blueberry Crisp

Prep 20 minutes   **Bake** 45 minutes
Makes 6 servings

QUICK-
SCRATCH

¾   cup plus 2 tablespoons granulated sugar
1   tablespoon cornstarch
5   cups sliced, peeled peaches*
2   cups blueberries*
¼   cup apricot preserves
1¼   cups all-purpose flour
½   cup packed brown sugar, *C&H®*
½   teaspoon ground cinnamon, *McCormick®*
¼   teaspoon ground nutmeg, *McCormick®*
1   pinch salt
½   stick (¼ cup) plus 2 tablespoons butter, cut into pieces
¾   cup sliced almonds
2   teaspoons vanilla, *McCormick®*
     Whipped cream

1. Preheat oven to 375 degrees F. Grease and flour a 2½-quart rectangular baking dish.

2. In a small bowl, combine ½ cup of the granulated sugar and the cornstarch. In a large bowl, combine peaches and blueberries. Add preserves and the sugar mixture; stir until combined. Pour into prepared baking dish.

3. In a large bowl, combine flour, brown sugar, the remaining 6 tablespoons granulated sugar, the cinnamon, nutmeg, and salt. Add butter pieces; rub in with your fingers until mixture is in small lumps. Add almonds and vanilla and continue to work until you have a sandy mixture with small lumps. Sprinkle over top of fruit mixture in pan.

4. Bake in preheated oven for 45 to 50 minutes or until fruit is bubbling. Serve warm. Serve with whipped cream.

*NOTE: If using frozen fruit, decrease the sugar added to fruit to ¼ cup and increase the cornstarch to 3 tablespoons.

Apple Ginger Crisp

Prep 20 minutes   **Bake** 50 minutes
Makes 10 servings

	Nonstick vegetable cooking spray, *Pam*®
2	**packages (14 ounces each) sliced green apples, *Chiquita*®**
½	**cup plus 3 tablespoons glazed pecans, chopped, *Emerald*®**
½	**cup packed brown sugar, *C&H*®**
¼	**cup apple butter, *Tropical*®**
3	**tablespoons crystallized ginger, chopped, *Dynasty*®**
2	**tablespoons lemon juice, *Minute Maid*®**
¼	**teaspoon ground ginger, *McCormick*®**
2	**cups ginger snaps, *Archway*®**
½	**stick (¼ cup) cold butter, cut into small pieces**
1	**tablespoon all-purpose flour**

1. Preheat oven to 350 degrees F. Spray a 2½-quart casserole with cooking spray.

2. In a large bowl, combine apples, 3 tablespoons of the glazed pecans, the brown sugar, apple butter, crystallized ginger, lemon juice, and ground ginger. Spoon into prepared casserole; set aside.

3. Place ginger snaps in a large zip-top bag. Press out air and seal. Roll over with a rolling pin until crushed. Transfer to a medium bowl and toss with the remaining ½ cup pecans, the butter pieces, and flour. Spoon over apple mixture.

4. Bake in preheated oven for 50 to 60 minutes or until bubbling and fruit is tender. Serve warm.

SERVING IDEA: Serve with scoops of vanilla bean ice cream.

Walnut Coffee Cake

Prep 25 minutes   **Bake** 45 minutes
Makes 10 servings

QUICK-
SCRATCH

STREUSEL TOPPING:
1   cup chopped walnuts
¾   cup packed brown sugar, *C&H*®
¼   cup golden raisins, chopped, *Sun-Maid*®
1   tablespoon ground cinnamon, *McCormick*®
1   teaspoon unsweetened cocoa powder, *Hershey's*®

BUTTERMILK CAKE:
3   cups all-purpose flour
2   teaspoons baking powder
1   teaspoon baking soda
¼   teaspoon salt
1⅔   cups granulated sugar
2   sticks (1 cup) butter, softened
4   eggs
1   cup buttermilk

1. For Streusel Topping, in a small bowl, combine walnuts, brown sugar, raisins, cinnamon, and cocoa powder.

2. For Buttermilk Cake, preheat oven to 375 degrees F. Grease and flour a fluted tube pan and set aside.

3. In a medium bowl, sift together flour, baking powder, baking soda, and salt; set aside.

4. In a large bowl, combine sugar and butter; beat with an electric mixer on medium speed until light and fluffy. Add eggs, one at a time, beating well after each addition. Alternately add flour mixture and buttermilk to butter mixture, beating just until combined.

5. Sprinkle one-third of the topping into prepared pan. Pour half of the cake batter over. Repeat layering topping and batter, ending with the last one-third of the topping.

6. Bake in preheated oven for 45 to 50 minutes or until wooden pick inserted in center of cake comes out clean. Cool in pan on wire rack for 30 minutes. Turn cake pan over onto serving plate and gently lift pan to remove cake. Serve warm.

Cranberry Coffee Cake

Prep 15 minutes   **Bake** 40 minutes
Makes 9 servings

Nonstick butter-flavor cooking spray, *Pam®*
1   package (15-ounce) cranberry quick bread mix, *Krusteaz®*
¾   cup sour cream
½   cup white cranberry juice, *Ocean Spray®*
¼   cup vegetable oil, *Crisco®*
2   eggs
½   cup sugar
¼   cup all-purpose flour
¼   cup pecans, finely chopped
3   tablespoons cold butter, cut into tiny pieces

1. Preheat oven to 350 degrees F. Spray a 9×9-inch baking pan with cooking spray and set aside.

2. In a large bowl, combine quick bread mix, sour cream, white cranberry juice, oil, and eggs, stirring with a wooden spoon until mixed. Pour into prepared pan.

3. In a small bowl, combine sugar, flour, and pecans. Add butter pieces and rub in with your fingers until mixture is crumbly. Sprinkle over cake batter.

4. Bake in preheated oven for 40 to 45 minutes or until wooden pick inserted in center comes out clean. Cool in pan on a wire rack.

Strawberry Shortcake

Prep 30 minutes   **Bake** 15 minutes
Chill 1 hour   **Makes** 6 servings

1½	pounds fresh strawberries, hulled and sliced
¾	cup granulated sugar
1⅔	cups whipping cream
1	egg
2½	teaspoons vanilla, *McCormick*®
2	cups self-rising flour
1	pinch salt
1	stick (½ cup) cold butter, cut into pieces

1. In a medium bowl, combine strawberries and 6 tablespoons of the granulated sugar. Chill in refrigerator for at least 1 hour.

2. Preheat oven to 450 degrees F. Line a baking sheet with parchment paper. In a small bowl, whisk together ⅔ cup of the whipping cream, the egg, and 2 teaspoons of the vanilla; set aside.

3. In a medium bowl, sift together the self-rising flour, the remaining 2 tablespoons sugar, and the salt. Add butter pieces; rub with your fingers until mixture is in fine crumbs. Add whipping cream mixture and stir until dough comes together.

4. On a baking sheet, using your fingertips, pat dough into a ¾-inch-thick rectangle. Bake in preheated oven for 15 to 20 minutes or until lightly browned on bottom. Transfer to a wire rack and let cool. Using a sharp knife, cut into 6 equal pieces.

5. In a large bowl, beat the remaining 1 cup whipping cream with an electric mixer on medium speed about 2 minutes or until thickened. Add the remaining ¼ cup sugar, 1 tablespoon at a time, and the remaining ½ teaspoon vanilla; continue to beat on high speed until soft peaks form.

6. To serve, split each cooled shortcake and place bottoms on serving plates. Spoon strawberries and accumulated juices over shortcakes. Place shortcake tops on strawberries. Top each with whipped cream.

Piña Colada Shortcake

Prep 25 minutes   **Bake** 6 minutes
Makes 8 servings

¼   cup shredded coconut
3   cans (8 ounces each) pineapple chunks in juice, drained and juice
      reserved, *Dole*®
¾   cup cream of coconut, *Coco Lopez*® *
2   (10-ounce) frozen pound cakes, thawed, *Sara Lee*®
1   teaspoon rum extract, *McCormick*®
1   container (8-ounce) frozen whipped topping, thawed, *Cool Whip*®
5   tablespoons packed brown sugar, *C&H*®
2   tablespoons butter
¼   teaspoon ground allspice, *McCormick*®

1. Preheat oven to 350 degrees F. Spread coconut on a baking sheet. Toast in preheated oven for 6 to 8 minutes or until golden brown.

2. In a small bowl, combine half of the reserved pineapple juice and the cream of coconut. Using a wooden skewer, poke holes over entire top of the pound cakes. Pour coconut-pineapple juice mixture over top of the cakes. Let stand until all of the liquid is absorbed.

3. Stir rum extract into whipped topping and set aside.

4. In a medium saucepan, combine brown sugar and butter; cook and stir over medium-high heat until melted. Add drained pineapple chunks and allspice. Cook and stir until pineapple is caramelized. Using a slotted spoon, transfer pineapple chunks to a medium bowl and set aside. Add the remaining reserved pineapple juice to saucepan. Bring to boiling; boil until liquid is reduced by half. Remove from heat.

5. Cut each pound cake into 8 slices. To serve, place 8 of the cake slices on serving plates. Spoon pineapple chunks and juice mixture over cake on plates. Top with remaining cake slices. Top with whipped topping mixture; sprinkle with toasted coconut.

*NOTE: Cream of coconut is a nonalcoholic drink mixer that can be found in the liquor section of the supermarket.

New York-Style Cheesecake

Prep 25 minutes
Bake 1 hour 30 minutes
Chill 6 hours   **Makes** 10 servings

QUICK-SCRATCH

WAFER CRUST:
Nonstick vegetable cooking spray, *Pam*®
2   cups vanilla wafer cookies, *Nilla*®
2   tablespoons sugar
6   tablespoons butter, melted

FILLING:
4   packages (8 ounces each) cream cheese, softened, *Philadelphia*®
1⅓   cups sugar
3   tablespoons all-purpose flour
1   pinch salt
5   eggs, room temperature
⅓   cup whipping cream, room temperature
1½   teaspoons vanilla, *McCormick*®
¼   teaspoon ground nutmeg, *McCormick*®

SOUR CREAM TOPPING:
1   cup sour cream
3   tablespoons sugar
1   teaspoon vanilla, *McCormick*®
       Fresh fruit (optional)

1. For Wafer Crust, spray 9-inch springform pan with cooking spray. Place on baking sheet.

2. In a food processor, combine vanilla wafer cookies and sugar; cover and process until in fine crumbs. Add butter and pulse until mixture comes together. Press crumb mixture into bottom of prepared springform pan. Chill in refrigerator until ready to use.

3. For Filling, preheat oven to 350 degrees F. Place cream cheese in the bowl of a standing mixer with paddle attachment; beat on lowest speed until smooth. Add sugar, flour, and salt; beat until smooth. Add eggs, one at a time, beating well after each addition. Using a rubber spatula, scrape down sides of the bowl and add cream, vanilla, and nutmeg. Beat until combined. Pour onto prepared crumb crust.

4. Bake in preheated oven for 15 minutes. Reduce temperature to 250 degrees F and continue to bake about 60 to 80 minutes or until set with a wet-looking center.

5. For Sour Cream Topping, in a small bowl, combine sour cream, sugar, and vanilla; stir until smooth. Remove cheesecake from oven and pour Topping over still-warm cheesecake. Bake for 15 to 20 minutes more or until topping is set.

6. Cool in pan on a wire rack. Chill in refrigerator for at least 6 hours. Remove from pan just before serving. Top with fresh fruit (optional).

Cherry Fudge Cheesecake

Prep 15 minutes   **Bake** 55 minutes
Makes 8 servings

	Nonstick spray for baking, *Pam*®
1	**package (21-ounce) fudge supreme brownie mix, *Betty Crocker*®**
1	**stick (½ cup) butter, melted**
2	**packages (8 ounces each) cream cheese, softened, *Philadelphia*®**
¼	**cup sugar**
2	**eggs**
1	**can (21-ounce) cherry pie filling, *Comstock*® *More Fruit* or *Wilderness*® *More Fruit***
½	**cup fudge topping, *Mrs. Richardson's*®**

1. Preheat oven to 350 degrees F. Spray a 9-inch springform pan with nonstick spray.

2. In a medium bowl, stir together brownie mix and melted butter until mixture comes together. Lightly press mixture into bottom and part way up the sides of the springform pan; set aside.

3. In a large bowl, combine cream cheese and sugar; beat with an electric mixer on medium speed until smooth. Add eggs, one at a time, beating well after each addition. Stir in cherry pie filling. Pour into prepared brownie crust.

4. Pour fudge topping into a small microwave-safe bowl; microwave on high setting (100 percent power) for 20 seconds. Drop spoonfuls of the fudge topping over the cheesecake; swirl with a knife.

5. Bake in preheated oven for 55 to 60 minutes or until set in center. Cool in pan on a wire rack. Remove from pan and serve at room temperature or chill before serving.

Éclairs

Prep 45 minutes   **Bake** 27 minutes
Makes 26 éclairs

QUICK-SCRATCH

⅔	cup all-purpose flour, sifted
2	tablespoons cornstarch
4	cups milk
12	egg yolks
1	cup sugar
1	vanilla bean, split and scraped
¼	cup butter
1	teaspoon vanilla, *McCormick®*
1	recipe Pâte à Choux (see recipe, page 98)
1	egg
1	teaspoon water
10	ounces semisweet chocolate baking bar, chopped, *Baker's®*
1	cup whipping cream
1	tablespoon light-color corn syrup, *Karo®*

1. For pastry cream, in a medium bowl, stir together flour and cornstarch. Add 1 cup of the milk and the egg yolks; stir to make a paste. Set aside. In a large saucepan, combine the remaining 3 cups milk, the sugar, and the vanilla bean. Heat over medium-high heat just until boiling. Remove from heat. Slowly pour one-fourth of the warmed milk into the paste mixture, whisking constantly; pour back into saucepan. Return to heat; cook and stir for 3 to 5 minutes or until mixture thickens. Remove from heat and pour into a large bowl. Remove vanilla bean. Stir in butter and vanilla extract until smooth. Cool to room temperature; chill until ready to use.

2. For Éclairs, preheat oven to 425 degrees F. Line 2 baking sheets with parchment paper; set aside. Fill a deep roasting pan with boiling water and place at bottom of the oven. Prepare Pâte à Choux. Insert a large round tip into a large pastry bag and fill with Pâte à Choux. Twist and secure top. Pipe dough into 4-inch-long straight lines on prepared baking sheets, spacing at least 1 inch apart.

3. In a small bowl, lightly whisk together egg and the water to make an egg wash. Using a pastry brush, brush dough with the egg wash. Bake in preheated oven for 15 to 20 minutes or until puffed and golden brown. Rotate baking sheets, reduce temperature to 350 degrees F and prop oven door open slightly. Bake for 12 to 20 minutes more or until dry to the touch and light in weight. Cool on baking sheets on wire racks.

4. For Ganache, place chocolate in a medium bowl; set aside. In a small saucepan, combine whipping cream and corn syrup; cook and stir over medium heat just until boiling. Pour cream mixture over chocolate; using a rubber spatula, stir until completely smooth.

5. To serve, cut top off each Éclair. Spread some of the Ganache on top side of each Éclair. Sit upright on flat surface to set. Fill the centers of each Éclair bottom with pastry cream. Place tops back on filled Éclair bottoms. Serve immediately or keep refrigerated until ready to serve.

NOTE: If desired, fill Éclairs with sweetened whipped cream or whipped topping instead of Pastry Cream.

Pâte à Choux

Prep 20 minutes   **Bake** 27 minutes
Makes enough dough for 26 Éclairs

2   sticks (1 cup) butter
½   cup water
½   cup milk
2   cups plus 2 tablespoons all-purpose flour
¼   teaspoon salt
8   to 10 eggs

1. Preheat oven to 425 degrees F. Fill a deep roasting pan with boiling water and place at bottom of the oven. Lightly grease a baking sheet or line baking sheet with parchment paper.

2. In a medium saucepan, combine butter, the water, and milk; cook over medium heat until boiling. Remove from heat and sift in flour and salt. Cook for 4 minutes more, stirring constantly with a wooden spoon. Transfer to a large bowl.

3. Add eggs, one at a time, stirring well after each addition. After the eighth egg is stirred in, check consistency of dough. If it is sticky and stretchy when you lift spoon high in the air, stop adding eggs. If it breaks, add the remaining eggs and stir until stretchy and well mixed.

4. Use a pastry bag to pipe into Éclair shapes (see page 96) or place heaping tablespoons of dough on baking sheet. Bake in preheated oven for 15 to 20 minutes or until puffed and golden brown. Rotate baking sheets, reduce temperature to 350 degrees F and prop oven door open slightly. Bake for 12 to 20 minutes more or until dry to the touch and light in weight. Cool on baking sheets on wire racks. Use for Éclair recipe or fill with ice cream, whipped cream, or other desired filling.

Ice Cream Profiteroles

Prep 25 minutes **Bake** 12 minutes
Makes 14 profiteroles

1	sheet frozen puff pastry, thawed, *Pepperidge Farm*®
1	cup semisweet chocolate chips, *Nestlé*®
½	cup whipping cream
½	cup caramel topping, *Smucker's*®
3½	cups vanilla bean ice cream, *Dreyer's*®
¾	cup pistachios, chopped

1. Preheat oven to 400 degrees F. For pastry puffs, unroll puff pastry on a lightly floured surface. Using a 2½-inch round cutter, cut circles from puff pastry. Reroll dough scraps and cut to make a total of 14 circles. Place pastry circles on ungreased baking sheets, spacing circles 1 inch apart.

2. Bake in preheated oven for 12 to 15 minutes or until puffed and golden brown. Transfer to a wire rack and let cool.

3. For chocolate-caramel sauce, place chocolate chips in a medium bowl; set aside. In a small saucepan, combine whipping cream and caramel topping. Cook and stir over medium heat until almost boiling. Pour over chocolate chips; using a rubber spatula, stir until completely smooth.

4. To serve, split or cut a pastry puff in half horizontally and place bottom half on a serving plate. Top with about ¼ cup of the ice cream; top with top half of the pastry puff. Drizzle with chocolate-caramel sauce and sprinkle with pistachios. Repeat with the remaining puffs, ice cream, chocolate-caramel sauce, and pistachios. Serve immediately.

Sandy's Sandies

1. Coat in sugar. To make a dressier version, sift powdered sugar or cocoa powder over warm sandies. Serve on a silver tray to add a touch of class to any occasion.

2. Add some crunch. Place Sandies in a zip-top bag, press out the air and seal. Roll over them with a rolling pin to crumble and you have a crunchy garnish for pudding, ice cream or whipped cream.

3. Candy surprise. Make Surprise Sandies by placing a piece of chocolate or candy in the center of each cookie immediately after they are removed from the oven.

4. Gift in a jar. Layer the premeasured dry ingredients for Mexican Chocolate Sandies in pretty jars and tie a recipe card and bow on each. You'll always have a ready gift or a quick dessert at your fingertips.

5. Stamp-in style. Use a cookie stamp to emboss a design on top of Quick-Scratch Sandies. Serve them on a pedestal to play up their elegance.

The Recipes

Lavender-Scented Sandies

Prep 25 minutes   **Bake** 8 minutes per batch
Cool 5 minutes   **Chill** 2 hours
Makes 28 (2½- to 3-inch) cookies

¼	cup sugar
2	teaspoons culinary lavender*
1	pouch (17.5-ounce) sugar cookie mix, *Betty Crocker®*
1	stick (½ cup) butter
1	egg
1	teaspoon finely shredded lemon zest

1. Preheat oven to 350 degrees F. Line 2 cookie sheets with parchment paper and set aside. In a food processor, combine sugar and lavender; cover and pulse about 20 seconds or until mixture is a fine powder.

2. In a large bowl, combine sugar mixture, cookie mix, butter, egg, and lemon zest; stir until dough forms. Turn out dough onto a lightly floured surface. Divide dough in half. Using your hands, shape each half into a 7-inch-long square-sided log. Wrap logs separately with plastic wrap and chill in refrigerator for at least 2 hours.

3. Remove 1 of the dough logs from refrigerator and cut into ½-inch-thick slices. Place half of the slices on each cookie sheet, spacing evenly. Bake in preheated oven for 8 to 10 minutes or until edges are golden brown. Cool on cookie sheets for 5 minutes. Transfer cookies to a wire rack; let cool. Repeat with remaining dough log.

*NOTE: Look for edible lavender at gourmet stores or purchase online.

Quick-Scratch Sandies

Prep 20 minutes   **Bake** 8 minutes per batch
Cool 5 minutes   **Chill** 1 hour
Makes about 24 (2¾-inch) cookies

1¾	cups all-purpose flour
¾	cup sugar
1	pinch salt
1½	sticks (¾ cup) cold butter, cut into small pieces
1	egg yolk
2	tablespoons whipping cream
2	teaspoons vanilla, *McCormick®*

1. Preheat oven to 350 degrees F. Line 2 cookie sheets with parchment paper. In a food processor, combine flour, sugar, and salt. Add cold butter pieces; cover and pulse until mixture is crumbly. In a small bowl, whisk together egg yolk, whipping cream, and vanilla. Add to mixture in food processor; pulse until dough starts to come together.

2. Turn out dough on a flat working surface. Using your hands, shape dough into a log 2 inches in diameter. Wrap log in plastic wrap and chill for 1 hour.

3. Cut log into ½-inch-thick slices. Place slices on prepared cookie sheets, spacing evenly. Bake in preheated oven for 8 to 10 minutes or until edges are lightly browned. Cool on cookie sheets for 5 minutes. Transfer cookies to wire racks; let cool.

Mexican Chocolate Sandies

Prep 20 minutes
Bake 10 minutes plus 18 minutes per batch
Cool 5 minutes   **Makes** 20 (2½-inch) cookies

¾	cup sliced almonds, *Planters®*
1	pouch (17.5-ounce) sugar cookie mix, *Betty Crocker®*
¼	cup packed brown sugar, *C&H®*
¼	cup unsweetened cocoa powder, *Hershey's®*
1	tablespoon ground cinnamon, *McCormick®*
½	stick (¼ cup) butter, softened
¼	cup butter-flavored shortening, *Crisco®*
1	egg
¾	cup bittersweet chocolate chips, chopped, *Ghirardelli®*

1. Preheat oven to 375 degrees F. Spread a thin, even layer of the almonds on a cookie sheet. Bake in preheated oven about 10 minutes or until almonds are lightly toasted. Remove from cookie sheet and cool completely.

2. Place cooled almonds in a medium zip-top bag. Press out air and seal. Using a rolling pin, roll over almonds until crushed; set aside.

3. Preheat oven to 350 degrees F. Line 2 cookie sheets with parchment paper. In a large bowl, combine cookie mix, brown sugar, cocoa powder, and cinnamon. Add butter, shortening, and egg; stir until dough forms. Stir in toasted almonds and chocolate chips.

4. Using your hands, roll 2 tablespoons of the dough into a ball and place on prepared cookie sheet. Press ball with the bottom of a drinking glass to flatten. Repeat with remaining dough, spacing evenly on cookie sheets.

5. Bake in preheated oven for 18 to 22 minutes or until edges are lightly browned. Cool on cookie sheets for 5 minutes. Transfer cookies to wire racks; let cool.

Lemon-Rosemary Sandies

Prep 20 minutes   **Bake** 10 minutes per batch
Cool 5 minutes   **Makes** 34 (3-inch) cookies

¼	cup sugar
2½	teaspoons dried rosemary leaves, *McCormick*®
1	egg
2	teaspoons lemon extract, *McCormick*®
1	pouch (17.5-ounce) sugar cookie mix, *Betty Crocker*®
1	stick (½ cup) butter, softened
	Sugar

1. Preheat oven to 350 degrees F. Line 2 cookie sheets with parchment paper. In a food processor, combine sugar and dried rosemary; cover and pulse until well mixed.

2. In a small bowl, whisk together egg and lemon extract. In a large bowl, combine cookie mix, butter, and sugar mixture. Add egg mixture and stir until dough forms.

3. Using your hands, roll 1 tablespoon of the dough into a ball; roll in additional sugar. Place on prepared cookie sheet. Repeat with remaining dough, spacing evenly on cookie sheets.

4. Bake in preheated oven for 10 to 12 minutes or until edges are lightly browned. Cool on cookie sheets for 5 minutes. Transfer cookies to wire racks; let cool.

Hello Sandies!

Prep 15 minutes   **Bake** 35 minutes
Makes 15 bars

26	pecan shortbread cookies, *Pecan Sandies*®
1	stick (½ cup) butter
1	cup pecans, chopped, *Planters*®
¾	cup butterscotch chips, *Nestlé*®
½	cup white baking chips, *Nestlé*®
½	cup semisweet chocolate chips, *Nestlé*®
2	cups sweetened flaked coconut, *Baker's*®
1	cup sweetened condensed milk, *Eagle Brand*®

1. Preheat oven to 325 degrees F. Place shortbread cookies in a food processor; cover and process until in fine crumbs. Add butter; pulse until mixture comes together. Press mixture into bottom of a 9×13-inch baking pan.

2. Sprinkle pecans over shortbread crust. Top with butterscotch chips, white baking chips, and chocolate chips. Sprinkle with coconut. Pour sweetened condensed milk evenly over entire mixture.

3. Bake in preheated oven for 35 to 40 minutes or until edges start to brown. Cool in pan on wire rack. Cut into bars.

Cherry Sandy Crumble

Prep 15 minutes   Bake 30 minutes
Makes 8 servings

2   cups frozen dark sweet cherries, thawed, *Dole®*
1   can (21-ounce) cherry pie filling, *Comstock® More Fruit*
1   package (5-ounce) dried tart and sweet cherries, *Sunsweet®*
½   cup granulated sugar
1   tablespoon quick-cooking tapioca, *Minute®*
10   pecan shortbread cookies, *Pecan Sandies®*
⅓   cup old-fashioned rolled oats, *Quaker®*
3   tablespoons packed brown sugar, *C&H®*
5   tablespoons butter, melted

1. Preheat oven to 375 degrees F. In a large bowl, combine thawed cherries, pie filling, dried cherries, granulated sugar, and tapioca; stir until well mixed. Pour into 1½-quart casserole.

2. In a food processor, combine shortbread cookies, oats, and brown sugar; cover and process until mixture is fine crumbs. Add butter; pulse about 10 seconds or until mixture comes together. Crumble over the top of the cherry mixture. Bake in preheated oven for 30 to 40 minutes or until top is golden brown and fruit is bubbly.

Sandy's Caramel-Praline Cheesecake

Prep 35 minutes   **Bake** 40 minutes
Makes 10 servings

	Nonstick vegetable cooking spray, *Pam*®
16	**pecan shortbread cookies, *Pecan Sandies*®**
¼	**cup plus 30 whole almonds, *Planters*®**
½	**stick (¼ cup) butter, melted**
6	**tablespoons sugar**
2	**tablespoons cake flour, *Swans Down*®**
¼	**teaspoon salt**
2	**packages (8 ounces each) cream cheese, softened, *Philadelphia*®**
4	**eggs**
1	**can (12.5-ounce) almond cake and pastry filling, *Solo*®**
30	**individually wrapped caramels, *Kraft*®**
1	**tablespoon whipping cream**

1. Preheat oven to 350 degrees F. Spray a 9-inch springform pan with cooking spray.

2. In a food processor, combine shortbread cookies and ¼ cup of the almonds; cover and process until mixture is fine crumbs. Add butter; pulse until mixture comes together. Press crumb mixture onto bottom of springform pan; set aside.

3. In a small bowl, combine sugar, cake flour, and salt; set aside. In a large bowl, beat cream cheese with an electric mixer on medium speed until smooth. Add eggs, one at a time, beating well after each addition. Add almond filling; beat until combined. Add flour mixture; beat until smooth. Pour over prepared crumb crust.

4. Bake in preheated oven for 40 to 45 minutes or until set in center. Cool in pan on a wire rack. Remove sides of pan. Chill in refrigerator until ready to serve.

5. To make pralines, unwrap caramels. In a large microwave-safe bowl, combine caramels and whipping cream; microwave on medium setting (50 percent power) for 2 minutes, stirring every 30 seconds. Drop 3 whole almonds into caramel; remove with spoon and drop onto a silicone baking mat. Repeat with remaining almonds, 3 at a time, to make 10 pralines. (Reheat caramel as needed if it becomes too hard to spoon out almonds.) Chill in refrigerator until hard.

6. Place pralines around outer edge of cheesecake, spacing evenly. Serve at room temperature or chilled.

Sandy's Apple Crumble Pie

Prep 15 minutes   **Bake** 50 minutes
Makes 8 servings

1	(9-inch) frozen deep-dish pie shell, thawed, *Marie Callendar's*®
12	pecan shortbread cookies, *Pecan Sandies*®
6	tablespoons pecan pieces, *Planters*®
¼	cup packed brown sugar, *C&H*®
1	teaspoon ground cinnamon, *McCormick*®
5	tablespoons butter, cut into pieces
1½	cans (21 ounces each) apple pie filling, *Comstock*® *More Fruit*
	Vanilla bean ice cream

1. Move oven rack to lowest position and preheat oven to 375 degrees F. Line a baking sheet with foil.

2. Using a fork, poke holes in bottom of the pie shell; bake in preheated oven for 15 minutes. Cool in pan on a wire rack.

3. In a food processor, combine shortbread cookies, pecans, brown sugar, and cinnamon; cover and process until mixture is fine crumbs. Add butter; pulse about 10 seconds or until mixture looks crumbly.

4. Pour apple pie filling into cooled crust. Pour pecan mixture evenly over apples. Bake in preheated oven for 35 to 40 minutes or until top is golden brown and fruit is bubbly. Serve warm or cooled to room temperature. Serve with vanilla bean ice cream.

Sandy's Pecan Pie Bars

Prep 20 minutes   **Bake** 35 minutes
Makes 12 bars

> Nonstick butter-flavor cooking spray, *Pam®*
> 24   pecan shortbread cookies, *Pecan Sandies®*
> 2   sticks (1 cup) butter
> 1¼   cups packed dark brown sugar, *C&H®*
> ⅓   cup light-color corn syrup, *Karo®*
> 2   tablespoons whipping cream
> 2   cups pecans, chopped, *Planters®*
> 1   teaspoon vanilla, *McCormick®*

1. Preheat oven to 350 degrees F. Spray a 9-inch square baking pan with cooking spray. Place shortbread cookies in a food processor; cover and pulse until in fine crumbs. Cut ½ cup of the butter into small pieces. Add butter pieces to crumbs in food processor. Cover and pulse until mixture comes together. Press crumb mixture into bottom of the prepared pan. Bake in preheated oven for 15 minutes. Cool in pan on a wire rack.

2. In a medium saucepan, combine the remaining ½ cup butter, the brown sugar, corn syrup, and whipping cream; cook and stir over medium-high heat just until boiling. Boil for 1 minute; remove from heat. Stir in pecans and vanilla. Pour pecan mixture over cooled shortbread crust. Bake in preheated oven about 20 minutes or until bubbling. Cool in pan on a wire rack. Cut into bars.

Cocoa Peanut Butter Pie

Prep 20 minutes   **Bake** 5 minutes
Stand 20 minutes   **Freeze** 2 hours
Makes 8 servings

> 12   pecan shortbread cookies, *Pecan Sandies®*
> ¼   cup packed brown sugar, *C&H®*
> ¼   cup unsweetened cocoa powder, *Hershey's®*
> ½   stick (¼ cup) butter, melted
> 4   ounces cream cheese, softened, *Philadelphia®*
> 1   cup powdered sugar, *C&H®*
> 1   cup creamy peanut butter, *Skippy® Natural*
> ½   cup milk
> 1   carton (8-ounce) frozen whipped topping, thawed, *Cool Whip®*
>   Miniature chocolate-covered peanut butter cups,
>   halved, *Reese's®* (optional)

1. Preheat oven to 350 degrees F. In a food processor, combine shortbread cookies, brown sugar, and cocoa powder; cover and process until mixture is fine crumbs. Add butter; pulse until mixture comes together. Press crumb mixture into bottom of a 9-inch pie plate. Bake in preheated oven for 5 to 7 minutes or until set. Cool in pie plate on a wire rack. In a large bowl, beat cream cheese with an electric mixer on low speed until fluffy. Add powdered sugar and peanut butter; beat until thick. Gradually add milk, beating until smooth.

2. Gently stir in whipped topping. Spread onto cooled crust. Cover with plastic wrap and freeze for 2 hours. Let stand at room temperature for 20 minutes before serving. Garnish with peanut butter cup halves (optional). (Store leftovers in refrigerator; do not return to freezer.)

Chocolate Confections

1. Chocolate dippin'. Add one tablespoon of vegetable shortening per cup of chocolate chips when melting chocolate for dipping or coating. The chocolate adheres easier and has a glossier sheen.

2. Freezer wrap. Double-wrap chocolates in airtight plastic bags and freeze for up to three months. To prevent condensation, thaw chocolates sealed in the bags until they return to room temperature.

3. A touch of gold. Dust fudge, truffles, and bonbons with edible gold glitter or non-toxic luster dust to give them a rich look. Serve on a gold charger or package them in frilly candy cups to give as gifts.

4. Shake to coat. Instead of hand-rolling candy balls in sugar or nuts, place them in the bowl with the sugar (or nuts) and gently shake the bowl to coat.

5. Finishing touch. Add drama with color. Sliced kiwi, raspberries, or orange slices look—and taste—delicious on a chocolate dessert.

The Recipes

Honey Chocolate Cake

Prep 30 minutes   **Bake** 40 minutes
Makes 10 servings

PEANUT FILLING:

2	cups frozen whipped topping, thawed, *Cool Whip*®
½	cup honey roasted peanuts, *Emerald*®
¼	cup dry instant vanilla pudding and pie filling, *Jell-O*®
2	tablespoons honey, *Sue Bee*®

HONEY CHOCOLATE CAKE:

	Nonstick spray for baking, *Pam*®
1	package (18.25-ounce) butter recipe chocolate cake mix, *Betty Crocker*®
1	cup low-fat chocolate milk, *Nesquik*®
1	stick (½ cup) butter, softened
3	eggs
¼	cup honey, *Sue Bee*®

HONEY CHOCOLATE ICING:

1	package (10-ounce) dark chocolate chips, *Nestlé*® *Chocolatier*
1	cup whipping cream
½	cup honey, *Sue Bee*®
	Fresh mint sprig (optional)

1. For Peanut Filling, in a medium bowl, combine whipped topping, peanuts, dry instant pudding, and honey, stirring until well mixed. Cover with plastic wrap and chill until ready to use.

2. For Honey Chocolate Cake, preheat oven to 350 degrees F. Spray two 8-inch round cake pans with nonstick spray.

3. In a large bowl, combine dry cake mix, chocolate milk, butter, eggs, and honey; beat with an electric mixer on low speed for 30 seconds. Using a rubber spatula, scrape down sides of bowl; beat for 2 minutes on medium speed. Pour batter into prepared cake pans.

4. Bake in preheated oven for 40 to 45 minutes or until wooden pick inserted in centers comes out clean. Cool cake layers in pans on wire racks for 10 minutes. Remove cake layers from pans.

5. For Honey Chocolate Icing, place chocolate chips in a medium bowl; set aside. In a small saucepan, combine whipping cream and honey; cook over medium heat just until boiling. Pour cream mixture over chocolate chips; stir with a rubber spatula until completely smooth. Cool to room temperature.

6. To assemble, place 1 of the cake layers on a serving plate. Spread Peanut Filling evenly over cake on serving plate; top with the other cake layer. Pour Honey Chocolate Icing over top of cake and use a knife to spread down sides of cake. If desired, garnish with mint sprig.

Chocolate-Hazelnut Cake

Prep 30 minutes   **Bake** 24 minutes
Makes 12 servings

	Nonstick spray for baking, *Pam*®
¾	**cup whole hazelnuts (filberts)**
1	**package (18.25-ounce) devil's food cake mix, *Betty Crocker*®**
1⅓	**cups root beer, *Barq's*®**
½	**cup vegetable oil, *Crisco*®**
4	**eggs**
½	**cup sour cream**
¼	**cup all-purpose flour**
¼	**cup unsweetened cocoa powder, *Hershey's*®**
¼	**cup dark chocolate chips, *Nestlé*® *Chocolatier***
1	**teaspoon vanilla extract, *McCormick*®**
1	**pinch kosher salt**
2	**cans (16 ounces each) chocolate frosting, *Betty Crocker*®**
1	**jar (13-ounce) chocolate-hazelnut spread, *Nutella*®**

1. Preheat oven to 350 degrees F. Spray two 9-inch round cake pans with cooking spray and set aside.

2. Place ½ cup of the hazelnuts in a food processor; cover and process until very finely chopped. Set aside.

3. In a large bowl, combine cake mix, root beer, oil, eggs, sour cream, flour, cocoa powder, and very finely chopped hazelnuts; beat with an electric mixer on low speed for 30 seconds. Using a rubber spatula, scrape down sides of bowl; beat on medium speed for 2 minutes more. Pour batter into prepared cake pans.

4. Bake in preheated oven for 24 to 28 minutes or until a wooden pick inserted in centers comes out clean. Cool in pans on wire racks.

5. Place chocolate chips in a small microwave-safe bowl. Microwave on medium setting (50 percent power) for 30 seconds; stir. Repeat microwaving in 30-second intervals until melted and smooth. Using the remaining ¼ cup hazelnuts, dip half of each nut into the melted chocolate. Place on plate and set aside.

6. Stir vanilla and salt into frosting; cover until ready to use. To assemble, place 1 of the cake layers on a serving plate; spread with an even layer of the chocolate-hazelnut spread. Top with the remaining cake layer. Frost with the chocolate frosting mixture and arrange chocolate-dipped hazelnuts on top.

Deep Dark Fudge Cake
with Pistachio Frosting

Prep 25 minutes   **Bake** 35 minutes
Makes 12 servings

FUDGE CAKE:
Nonstick spray for baking, *Pam*®
1   package (18.25-ounce) chocolate fudge cake mix, *Betty Crocker*®
1   cup low-fat chocolate milk, *Nesquik*®
1   cup fudge topping, *Mrs. Richardson's*®
½   cup vegetable oil, *Crisco*®
4   eggs
1½   cups dark chocolate chips, chopped, *Nestlé*® *Chocolatier*

PISTACHIO FROSTING:
1   cup milk
1   package (4-serving-size) instant pistachio pudding and pie filling, *Jell-O*®
1   jar (7-ounce) marshmallow creme, *Jet-Puffed*®
1   container (8-ounce) frozen whipped topping, thawed, *Cool Whip*®
     Pistachios, chopped

1. For Fudge Cake, preheat oven to 350 degrees F. Spray two 8-inch round cake pans with nonstick spray.

2. In a large bowl, combine cake mix, chocolate milk, fudge topping, oil, and eggs; beat with an electric mixer on low speed for 30 seconds. Using a rubber spatula, scrape down sides of bowl; beat on medium speed for 2 minutes. Stir in chocolate chips. Pour batter into prepared cake pans.

3. Bake in preheated oven for 35 to 45 minutes or until a wooden pick inserted in centers comes out clean. Cool cake layers in pans on wire racks for 10 minutes. Remove cake layers from pans. Cool completely on wire racks.

4. For Pistachio Frosting, in a large bowl, combine milk and dry instant pudding; whisk for 2 minutes. Let pudding mixture stand about 3 minutes or until thick. Add marshmallow creme; stir until well mixed. Stir in whipped topping.

5. Fill and frost cake layers with Pistachio Frosting. If desired, sprinkle with chopped pistachios.

Malt Ball Cupcakes

Prep 30 minutes   **Bake** 20 minutes
Makes 24 cupcakes

1	package (18.25-ounce) milk chocolate cake mix, *Betty Crocker*®
1	cup chocolate malted milk powder, *Carnation*®
1¼	cups cola, *Coca-Cola*®
⅓	cup vegetable oil, *Crisco*®
3	eggs
1¼	cups milk
1	package (4-serving-size) instant chocolate pudding and pie filling, *Jell-O*®
1	teaspoon vanilla, *McCormick*®
1	pinch salt
1½	containers (12 ounces each) milk chocolate whipped frosting, *Betty Crocker*®
24	malted milk balls, crushed, *Whoppers*®
	Pirouette cookie sticks

1. Preheat oven to 350 degrees F. Grease twenty-four 4-ounce oven-safe cups or line twenty-four 2½-inch muffin cups with paper baking cups.

2. In a large bowl, combine cake mix and ½ cup of the malted milk powder. Add cola, oil, and eggs; beat with an electric mixer on low speed for 30 seconds. Using a rubber spatula, scrape down sides of bowl and beat for 2 minutes on medium speed. Spoon batter into oven-safe cups or paper baking cups, filling each two-thirds full.

3. Bake in preheated oven for 20 to 25 minutes or until wooden pick inserted in centers comes out clean. Remove cupcakes from muffin cups, if using; cool on wire racks.

4. In a large bowl, combine milk, dry instant pudding, and the remaining ½ cup malted milk powder; whisk for 2 minutes. Let stand for 3 minutes or until thick.

5. Insert a wooden skewer into the center of a cooled cupcake, being careful not to touch the bottom of the cupcake; twist skewer to make a small hole. Repeat with the remaining cupcakes. Spoon pudding mixture into a pastry bag (if a pastry bag is not available, see tip, page 170) to fill hole with pudding. Wipe any excess pudding from top of cupcakes.

6. Stir vanilla and salt into frosting. Frost cupcakes and top with malted milk balls. Insert a pirouette cookie stick into each cupcake (optional).

Peppermint Patty Cupcakes

Prep 25 minutes   Bake 20 minutes
Cool 5 minutes   Makes 24 cupcakes

1	package (18.4-ounce) triple chocolate fudge mix, *Betty Crocker*®
1⅓	cups chocolate milk, *Hershey's*®
½	cup vegetable oil, *Crisco*®
3	eggs
2	teaspoons mint extract, *McCormick*®
1½	packages (10 ounces each) dark chocolate chips, *Nestlé*® *Chocolatier*
1½	cups whipping cream
24	chocolate-covered peppermint patties, *York*®

1. Preheat oven to 350 degrees F. Line twenty-four 2½-inch muffin cups with paper baking cups. In a large bowl, combine cake mix, chocolate milk, oil, eggs, and 1 teaspoon of the mint extract; beat with an electric mixer on low speed for 30 seconds. Scrape down sides of bowl; beat for 2 minutes on medium speed. Spoon batter into baking cups, filling each about two-thirds full. Insert one peppermint patty candy into each filled paper baking cup. Bake for 20 to 24 minutes or until wooden pick inserted comes out clean. Remove cupcakes from muffin cups; cool on wire racks.

2. Place chocolate chips in a medium microwave-safe bowl. In a small saucepan, combine whipping cream and the remaining 1 teaspoon mint extract; cook over medium heat just until boiling. Pour cream mixture over chocolate chips; stir until completely smooth. If not completely smooth, microwave on medium setting (50 percent power) for 2 minutes. Cool about 5 minutes or until mixture thickens. Dip cupcake tops into chocolate mixture; place cupcakes on wire racks. If necessary, use knife to smooth tops. Sprinkle with additional chopped peppermint patties (optional).

Almond Roca Fudge

Prep 25 minutes   Stand 4 hours
Makes 24 pieces

	Nonstick vegetable cooking spray, *Pam*®
2	cups sugar
1½	sticks (¾ cup) butter
⅔	cup evaporated milk, *Carnation*®
½	cup almond roca syrup, *Torani*®
2¾	cups semisweet chocolate chips, *Ghirardelli*®
1	jar (7-ounce) marshmallow creme, *Jet-Puffed*®
½	cup chopped sliced almonds, *Planters*®
¼	cup toffee bits, *Heath*®

1. Spray a 9×13-inch baking pan with cooking spray. In a medium saucepan, combine sugar, butter, evaporated milk, and almond roca syrup; cook over medium heat until mixture reaches a rolling boil, stirring occasionally. Clip a candy thermometer to the saucepan and cook about 10 minutes longer or until candy thermometer registers 235 degrees F, stirring constantly. Remove from heat. Stir in chocolate chips and marshmallow creme, stirring until smooth. Pour into prepared baking pan. Sprinkle almonds and toffee bits over top; lightly press into fudge. Let stand at room temperature about 4 hours or until set. Cut into pieces.

German Chocolate Cookies

Prep 20 minutes   **Bake** 12 minutes
Makes 10 cookie sandwiches

	Nonstick vegetable cooking spray, *Pam®*
1	**package (18.25-ounce) German chocolate cake mix,** *Betty Crocker®*
⅓	**cup chocolate milk**
½	**stick (¼ cup) butter, melted**
1	**egg**
½	**cup pecan pieces,** *Planters®*
½	**cup semisweet chocolate chips,** *Nestlé®*
½	**cup plus 2 tablespoons coconut pecan frosting,** *Betty Crocker®*

1. Preheat oven to 350 degrees F. Spray 2 cookie sheets with cooking spray.

2. In a large bowl, combine cake mix, chocolate milk, melted butter, and egg; beat with electric mixer on low speed for 1 minute. Stir in pecans and chocolate chips. Drop 2-tablespoon portions of the cookie dough onto prepared cookie sheets, spacing 2 inches apart.

3. Bake in preheated oven for 12 to 14 minutes or just until set in center, rotating cookie sheets halfway through baking time. Transfer cookies to wire rack; let cool.

4. Spread 1 tablespoon of the coconut pecan frosting on the bottom of a cookie; top with another cookie, bottom side down. Repeat to make 10 cookie sandwiches.

Chocolate-Nut Clusters

Prep 20 minutes   **Chill** 1 hour
Makes 12 to 16 clusters

	Nonstick vegetable cooking spray, *Pam®*
2	**bars (4 ounces each) semisweet baking chocolate, chopped,** *Ghirardelli®*
⅔	**cup sweetened condensed milk,** *Eagle Brand®*
16	**individual caramel candies, unwrapped,** *Kraft®*
1	**cup lightly salted mixed nuts,** *Planters®*

1. Spray a baking sheet with cooking spray. In a large microwave-safe bowl, combine chopped chocolate and sweetened condensed milk; microwave on medium setting (50 percent power) for 2½ minutes, stirring every 30 seconds. Add caramel candies to chocolate mixture; stir until melted. If not completely melted, microwave on medium setting (50 percent power) for 30-second intervals until melted. Stir in nuts.

2. Drop by heaping tablespoons onto prepared baking sheet. Chill about 1 hour or until set.

TO STORE: Place in airtight container. Store at room temperature for up to 3 days or in refrigerator for up to 1 week.

Chocolate-Hazelnut Truffles

Prep 20 minutes   **Chill** 4 hours
Makes 20 (1-tablespoon) truffles

2	**cups chocolate-hazelnut spread, *Nutella*®**
1	**cup powdered sugar, sifted, *C&H*®**
1	**cup hazelnuts (filberts), toasted and skins removed**

1. In a large bowl, combine chocolate-hazelnut spread and powdered sugar; beat with an electric mixer on low speed until well mixed. Cover with plastic wrap. Chill for 4 hours.

2. Place hazelnuts in a large zip-top bag. Press out air and seal. Using a rolling pin, pound and roll over hazelnuts until crushed.

3. Pour crushed hazelnuts into a pie plate. Scoop 1 tablespoon of the chocolate-hazelnut mixture; using slightly wet hands, form into a smooth ball. Roll ball in hazelnuts to coat entire ball and place on ungreased baking sheet. Repeat to make 20 truffles, rinsing hands when mixture becomes too sticky to roll. Chill until ready to serve.

TO STORE: Place truffles in an airtight container. Store in refrigerator for 1 week or in freezer for up to 3 months.

Swiss Orange Chocolate Truffles

Prep 25 minutes   **Chill** 2 hours
Makes 22 (1-tablespoon) truffles

1	**package (10-ounce) dark chocolate chips, *Nestlé*® *Chocolatier***
¾	**cup whipping cream**
3	**tablespoons orange juice concentrate, *Minute Maid*®**
2	**teaspoons grated orange zest (optional)**
2	**teaspoons pure orange extract, *McCormick*®**
3	**tablespoons unsweetened cocoa powder, *Hershey's*®**
	Grated orange zest (optional)

1. Place chocolate chips in a medium bowl; set aside. In a small saucepan, combine whipping cream and orange juice concentrate; cook over medium heat just until boiling. Pour cream mixture over chocolate chips; use a rubber spatula to stir until smooth. Stir in orange zest (optional) and orange extract. Cover with plastic wrap and chill for 2 hours.

2. Pour cocoa powder into a pie plate. Scoop 1 tablespoon of the chocolate mixture; using slightly wet hands, form into a ball. Roll ball in cocoa powder to coat entire ball and place on ungreased baking sheet. Repeat to make 22 truffles, rinsing hands when mixture becomes too sticky to roll. Chill until ready to serve. Sprinkle with grated orange zest (optional).

TO STORE: Place truffles in an airtight container. Store in refrigerator for up to 1 week or in freezer for up to 3 months.

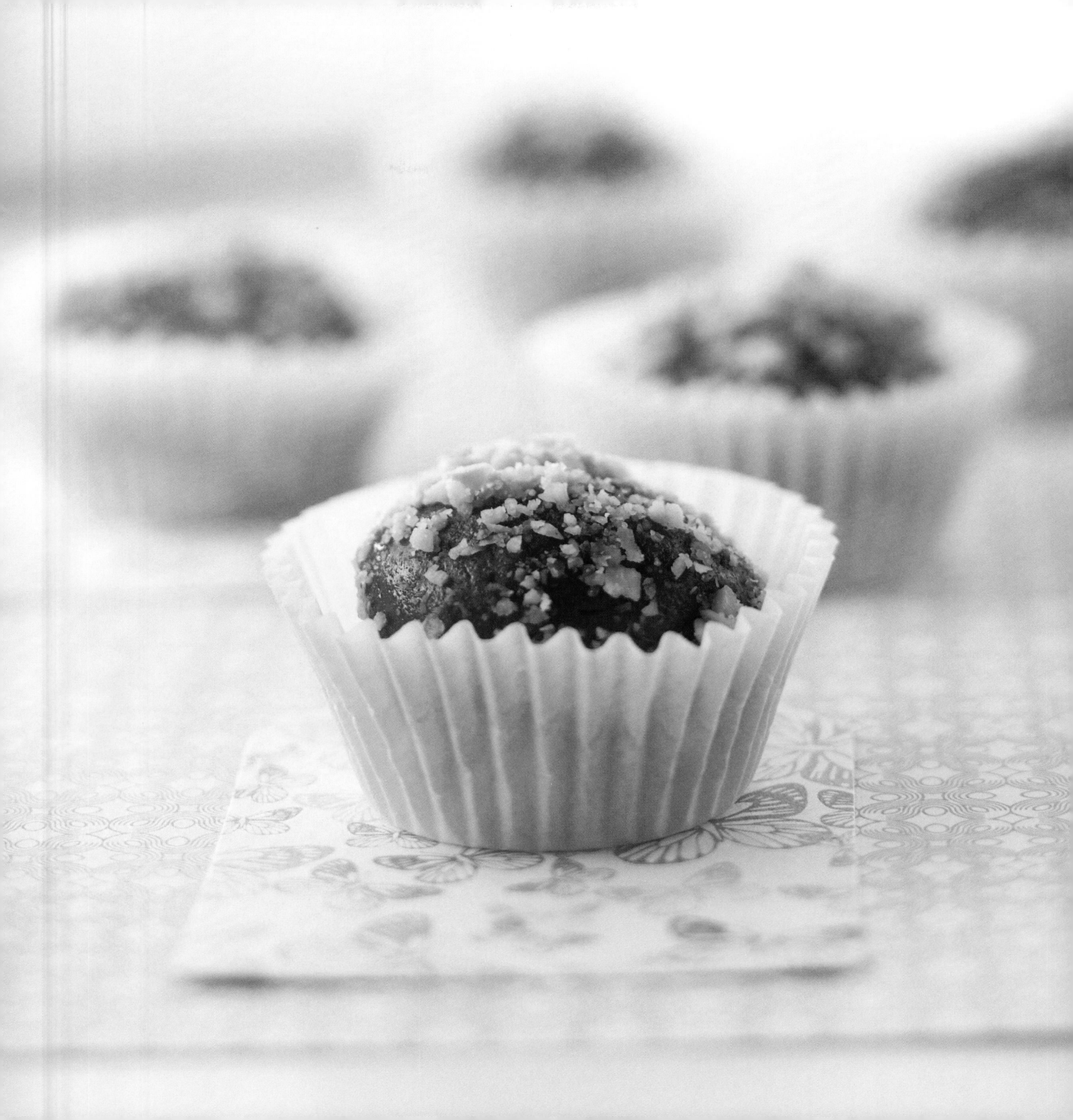

Chocolate-Raspberry Bark

Prep 20 minutes　Chill 3 hours
Makes 14 servings

Nonstick vegetable cooking spray, *Pam*®
1/4　cup red raspberry jam, *Smucker's*®
1　package (10-ounce) dark chocolate chips, *Nestlé*®
1　package (12-ounce) white baking chips, *Nestlé*®
2　ounces semisweet bar chocolate, chopped, *Nestlé*®
　Raspberry dessert topping, *Smucker's*® *Plate Scapers*®

1. Line a 9×13-inch baking pan with aluminum foil and spray with cooking spray. Place jam in a small microwave-safe bowl; microwave on high setting (100 percent power) for 45 seconds. Place dark chocolate chips in a medium microwave-safe bowl; microwave on medium setting (50 percent power) about 3 minutes or until smooth, stirring every 30 seconds. Quickly stir in heated jam, stirring until smooth. Immediately spread a thin, even layer of the chocolate-jam mixture in bottom of prepared baking pan. Chill about 1 hour or until firm.

2. Microwave white baking chips on medium setting (50 percent power) in a microwave-safe bowl for about 2 minutes or until smooth, stirring every 30 seconds. Spread a thin layer of the white mixture over dark chocolate in pan. Sprinkle chopped chocolate bar over white mixture. Drizzle dessert topping over top in desired pattern. Chill about 2 hours or until set. Lift foil from pan and break bark into pieces.

Holiday Bark

Prep 25 minutes　Chill 3 hours
Makes 16 servings

Nonstick vegetable cooking spray, *Pam*®
1　package (10-ounce) dark chocolate chips, *Nestlé*® *Chocolatier*
1　tablespoon vegetable oil, *Crisco*®
1　teaspoon pure peppermint extract, *McCormick*®
1　bar (8-ounce) white baking bar, chopped, *Ghirardelli*®
1/2　cup peppermint starlight mints
4　ounces white baking bar, chopped

1. Line a 9×13-inch baking pan with foil; spray with cooking spray; set aside. Microwave dark chocolate chips in a medium microwave-safe bowl; microwave on medium setting (50 percent power) for 3 minutes, stirring every 1½ minutes. In a bowl, stir together oil and peppermint extract. Pour half of the oil mixture into melted chocolate; spread a thin layer of the chocolate mixture in the bottom of the prepared baking pan. Chill about 1 hour or until set. Place starlight mints in a large zip-top bag. Press out air and seal. Pound candy with a rolling pin until crushed; set aside.

2. Place white baking bar in a small microwave-safe bowl; microwave on medium setting (50 percent power) for 2 minutes, stirring every 30 seconds. Add the remaining oil mixture to the melted white baking bar; stir until well mixed. Evenly spread a thin layer of the white mixture over dark chocolate layer in pan. Sprinkle crushed starlight mints over top and remaining 4 ounces chopped baking bar. Chill about 2 hours or until set. Break into pieces.

Embellish Me

1. Glam up the presentation. Stack champagne truffles in a champagne flute, serve mocha brownie bites in an espresso cup, rest a rum ball in a shot glass with a drizzle of liqueur.

2. Drizzles and drips. Use squeeze bottles to pinstripe a white plate with alternating stripes of fudge sauce and raspberry syrup. Finish with a double drizzle over ready-made cheesecake, bonbons, or tarts.

3. Beautiful toppings. Top store-bought desserts with crumbled cookies, crushed candy, or crystallized ginger to add another layer of color and taste.

4. A light dusting. Look to the pantry for creative dusting powders. A sprinkling of Pixy Stix®, flavored instant coffees, or cocoa powder make colorful garnishes.

5. Short-order shortcake. To make a speedy shortcake, horizontally slice a strawberry muffin in half. Spoon berries on the bottom half, add the top and garnish with whipped cream and a sprig of mint.

The Recipes

Lemony Layered Angel Food Cake

Start to Finish 20 minutes
Makes 10 servings

½   cup lemon curd, room temperature, *Dickinson's®*
1   container (12-ounce) whipped topping, *Cool Whip®*
5   to 8 drops yellow food coloring, *McCormick®*
1   (13-ounce) purchased angel food cake
¼   cup limoncello liqueur
      Lemon slices and lemon peel curls (optional)

1. Spoon lemon curd into a medium bowl; stir until smooth. Using a rubber spatula, fold in 1½ cups of the whipped topping and the food coloring until smooth. Using a long serrated knife, cut cake horizontally into thirds. Place bottom layer on a serving plate and brush with limoncello. Spread half of the lemon curd mixture on bottom layer and top with another cake layer. Brush layer with limoncello. Spread the remaining lemon curd mixture on middle layer and top with the remaining cake layer. Brush the remaining limoncello on top and sides of cake.

2. Frost top and sides of the cake with the remaining whipped topping. If desired, garnish with lemon slices. Serve immediately or refrigerate until ready to serve. Let stand at room temperature for 30 minutes before serving. Garnish with lemon slices and lemon peel curls (optional).

Neapolitan Angel Cake

Prep 25 minutes   **Freeze** 2 hours to 1 week
Makes 10 servings

1   (13-ounce) purchased angel food cake
1¼   cups chocolate ice cream, softened, *Häagen-Dazs®*
1   cup strawberry ice cream, softened, *Häagen-Dazs®*
¾   cup vanilla ice cream, softened, *Häagen-Dazs®*
1½   cups frozen whipped topping, thawed, *Cool Whip®*
1½   cups frozen strawberry whipped topping, thawed, *Cool Whip®*
¼   cup chocolate syrup, *Hershey's®*

1. Using a long serrated knife, cut cake horizontally into fourths. Place bottom layer on a serving plate. Scoop chocolate ice cream onto bottom layer and use a knife to spread evenly.* Top with second cake layer and spread with strawberry ice cream. Top with third cake layer and spread with vanilla ice cream. Top with last cake layer.

2. Freeze for at least 2 hours or up to 1 week before decorating and serving. Decorate top of cake with both whipped toppings. Drizzle chocolate syrup over cake and, if desired, garnish with fresh sliced *strawberries*. Drizzle with chocolate syrup. Slice and serve.

*NOTE: If the ice creams start to melt when assembling cake, place cake and ice creams in freezer until they are firm enough to work with again.

Christmas Cakes

Prep 15 minutes   Decorate 35 minutes
Makes 8 servings for each cake

CANDY CANE LANE CAKE:

2   cans (12 ounces each) whipped vanilla frosting, *Betty Crocker®*
2   8-inch purchased cake layers (any flavor)
     Christmas red gel food coloring
     White nonpareils
     Small candy canes
     Additional red-and-white candy decorations, *Wilton®*
     Decorating icing (white), *Betty Crocker® Easy Flow*
     Red-and-white mint candies

GINGERBREAD HOUSE CAKE:

2   cans (12 ounces each) whipped vanilla frosting, *Betty Crocker®*
2   8-inch purchased cake layers (any flavor)
     Leaf green gel food coloring
1   Mini Gingerbread House (page 152)
     Pretzels
     Holiday-theme candy cake decorations, *Wilton®*

SNOWMEN CAKE:

2   8-inch purchased cake layers (any flavor)
2   cans (12 ounces each) whipped fluffy white frosting, *Betty Crocker®*
     Sky blue gel food coloring, *Wilton®*
3   ice cream cones
8   large marshmallows, sliced in half crosswise
     Decorating icing (assorted colors), *Betty Crocker® Easy Flow*
     Holiday-theme candy cake decorations, *Wilton®*
     Powdered sugar

1. For Candy Cane Lane Cake, spread ½ cup of the frosting between cake layers. Color the remaining frosting with enough red gel food coloring to make desired color. Frost top and sides of cake. Make a candy cane lane on top of cake with white nonpareils. Line the lane with candy canes and other red-and-white candies. Pipe white decorating icing around base of cake. Garnish with star mint candies.

2. For Gingerbread House Cake, spread ½ cup of the frosting between cake layers. Color the remaining frosting with enough green gel food coloring to make desired color. Frost top and sides of cake. Place gingerbread house on top of cake. Decorate as desired with the remaining ingredients.

3. For Snowmen Cake, spread ½ cup of the frosting between cake layers. Color the remaining frosting with enough blue gel food coloring to make desired color. Frost top and sides of cake. For trees, place 3 inverted ice cream cones on cake. Along the sides of the cake, press two marshmallow halves into frosting to form one snowman. Repeat process to make 8 snowmen, spaced evenly around the cake base. Use decorating icing to make faces on snowmen. Decorate as desired with holiday-theme decorations. Just before serving, sift ice cream cones and cake top with powdered sugar.

Soda Fountain Cones

Prep 25 minutes   **Decorate** 20 minutes
Makes 12 cupcake cones

2	cups white baking chips, *Nestlé®*
1	box (2.75-ounce) ice cream cones, *Scoopy's® Jumbo Cups*
	Colored sanding sugar and/or colored sprinkles, *Cake Mate®*
4	cups whipped fluffy white frosting, *Betty Crocker®*
1	tablespoon strawberry extract, *McCormick®*
8	drops red food coloring, *McCormick®*
1	tablespoon root beer extract, *McCormick®*
	Brown gel food coloring, *Wilton®*
2	tablespoons frozen lemonade concentrate, thawed, *Minute Maid®*
2	tablespoons raspberry syrup, *Torani®*
12	to 15 drops blue food coloring, *McCormick®*
1½	cups jelly beans, *Jelly Belly®*
12	purchased cupcakes (any flavor), unfrosted

1. Place white baking chips in a medium microwave-safe bowl; microwave on medium setting (50 percent power) for 2½ minutes, stirring every 30 seconds.

2. Dip the collar of each ice cream cone in melted chips; if necessary, smooth with a knife. Hold each cone over a pie plate and sprinkle with colored sanding sugar and/or colored sprinkles. Place cones upside down on a baking sheet; let stand until chocolate hardens.

3. For strawberry frosting, place 1⅓ cups of the frosting in a small bowl; stir in the strawberry extract and red food coloring. For root beer frosting, place 1⅓ cups of the frosting in another small bowl; stir in the root beer extract and desired amount of brown food coloring. For blue raspberry frosting, place the remaining 1⅓ cups frosting in a medium bowl; stir in the lemonade concentrate, raspberry syrup, and blue food coloring.

4. Place 2 tablespoons of the jelly beans in the bottom of each cone. If necessary, remove paper cups from cupcakes; insert a cupcake upside down into the top of each cone. Frost each cupcake with one of the frosting flavors, swirling frosting in an upward pattern. Repeat to make twelve soda fountain cupcakes, frosting 4 cupcakes with each flavor of frosting.

Treasure Chest Cake

Prep 15 minutes   Chill 30 minutes
Decorate: 20 minutes   Makes 6 servings

1   (12-ounce) pound cake or loaf cake, *Entenmann's®*
1   can (12-ounce) whipped chocolate frosting, *Betty Crocker®*
    Brown sugar
    Assorted candies (such as chocolate gold coins, candy necklaces, ring
      pops, rip rolls, gummy rings, and/or Swedish fish)
    Decorating icing (desired colors), *Betty Crocker® Easy Flow*
    Green fruit roll-ups

1. Using a long serrated knife, cut pound cake in half horizontally. Place bottom of the cake on a serving plate. Frost cake top and sides with chocolate frosting. Refrigerate for 30 minutes to harden frosting.

2. Place assorted candies on frosted cake bottom. Place top of cake on candies. Decorate top and sides of treasure chest with assorted candies and/or icing. For sand, pour brown sugar onto serving plate around bottom of cake. For seaweed, cut green fruit roll-ups into strips; twist together and place at base of treasure chest. Decorate with additional candies.

Cheesecake Pops

Prep 30 minutes   Freeze 1½ hours
Makes 8 servings

1   (36-ounce) frozen key lime cheesecake, *Edward's®*
1   package (12-ounce) dark chocolate chips, *Nestlé® Chocolatier*
1   tablespoon shortening, *Crisco®*
    Nut topping, *Planters®*, or multi-color sprinkles (optional)

1. Line 2 baking sheets with parchment paper and set aside. Remove any topping from cheesecake and trim crust edge so it is flush with cake. Cut cheesecake into 8 slices and turn each slice on its side. Using the tip of a sharp knife, carefully make a small slit in the exact middle of each slice's crust. Carefully insert a wooden craft stick straight into each slice. Place on a prepared baking sheet and freeze for 30 minutes. (Store slices on their sides, if necessary.)

2. In a small saucepan, combine chocolate and shortening; cook over low heat, stirring constantly, about 1½ minutes or until most of the chocolate is melted. Remove from heat and stir until all chocolate is melted and smooth. Transfer chocolate to a large bowl and cool to room temperature.

3. Remove cheesecake slices from freezer. Grasp the wooden stick of a cheesecake slice and hold over the chocolate bowl. Using a large spoon in your other hand, pour chocolate over half of the cheesecake slice. Smooth out the chocolate and place on second prepared baking sheet. Repeat with remaining slices, working quickly. If desired, quickly sprinkle nut topping over chocolate. Freeze chocolate-covered slices for 1 hour.

White Chocolate Tartlets

Start to Finish 15 minutes
Makes 6 servings

1¾   cups milk
1   package (4-serving-size) instant white chocolate pudding and
        pie filling, *Jell-O®*
½   cup whipped cream cheese, softened, *Philadelphia®*
½   teaspoon vanilla, *McCormick®*
1   package (4-ounce) miniature graham cracker pie crusts, *Keebler®*
        Ready Crust®
      White baking bar and milk chocolate bar, shaved into curls
        (optional) (see tip, below)

1. In a large bowl, combine milk and pudding mix; whisk together for
2 minutes, then let stand about 3 minutes or until thick.

2. In a medium bowl, combine cream cheese and vanilla; beat with an
electric mixer on low speed until smooth. Add pudding and beat until
smooth.

3. Scoop 5 tablespoons of the cream cheese-pudding mixture into
each pie crust. If desired, garnish with chocolate shavings.

Pecan Pumpkin Pie

Start to Finish 10 minutes
Makes 6 servings

1   (24-ounce) purchased pumpkin pie
½   cup coconut pecan frosting, *Betty Crocker®*
⅓   cup pecans, chopped
¼   cup purchased fudge sauce
2   ounce semisweet chocolate bar, shaved into curls*
2   ounce white baking bar, shaved into curls*

1. Cut pumpkin pie into 6 slices. Add a spoonful of coconut frosting to
each pumpkin pie slice; sprinkle with pecans. Top with a spoonful of fudge
sauce. Sprinkle chocolate and white baking curls over fudge sauce.

*TIP: To shave chocolate bar into curls, gently draw a vegetable peeler across
one end of the chocolate bar.

Cheesecake with Chutney

1	cup mango and ginger chutney, *Truly Indian*®
½	cup apricot preserves, *Smucker's*® *Simply Fruit*®
¼	cup whole berry cranberry sauce, *Ocean Spray*®
¼	cup dried apricots, chopped, *Sun-Maid*®
¼	cup mango nectar, *Kern's*®
¼	teaspoon red pepper flakes
½	teaspoon orange extract, *McCormick*®
1	can (12-ounce) whipped cream frosting, *Betty Crocker*®
1	(10-inch) purchased cheesecake
1	(8-inch) purchased cheesecake
1	(6-inch) purchased cheesecake
	Fresh fruit, mint leaves, and sugared cranberries (optional)

1. In a large bowl, stir together chutney, preserves, cranberry sauce, chopped apricots, nectar, and red pepper flakes; set aside.

2. In a small bowl, stir orange extract into frosting. Frost each cheesecake layer with frosting. Place 10-inch cheesecake on a cake plate. Place the 8-inch layer of cheesecake on the center top of the 10-inch cheesecake. Place the 6-inch cheesecake on the center top of the 8-inch cheesecake.

3. Spoon chutney mixture over cheesecake layers. Garnish with fruit, mint, and cranberries (optional).

Brûlée Cheesecake

1	(30-ounce) frozen plain cheesecake, *Sara Lee*®
¼	cup packed brown sugar, *C&H*®
¼	cup granulated sugar
2	cups assorted fresh berries (strawberries, blueberries, raspberries, and/or blackberries), rinsed and patted dry

1. Let cheesecake stand on kitchen counter about 30 minutes or just until thawed.

2. Preheat broiler. Using a fine-mesh strainer, sprinkle both sugars over top of cheesecake.

3. Place cheesecake on a baking sheet. Broil 4 inches from the heat for 1 minute. Rotate baking sheet and broil for 1 to 2 minutes more or until sugars are dark brown and bubbling.

4. Serve immediately with fresh berries.

Mini Gingerbread Houses

Prep 25 minutes   Stand overnight
Decorate 20 minutes
Makes 4 mini houses

1   tube (6-ounce) white icing, *Cake Mate® Easy Squeeze*
32   2-part graham cracker squares, *Honey Maid®*
1   can (6.4-ounce) white icing, *Betty Crocker® Easy Flow*
     Variety of small candies for decorating

1. Using squeezable icing as glue, glue together 5 graham cracker squares to make a box without a top. Let icing harden for a few minutes.

2. To make roof supports, use a serrated knife to cut 1 graham cracker square in half. Using a long side of a cracker half as a base, cut cracker half into a triangle. Repeat with the other cracker half. Squeeze icing onto the long side of each triangle and attach to the top of the 2 opposite walls.

3. Squeeze icing onto the edges of the roof supports. To make the roof, use 2 more graham cracker squares attached together with icing. Gently place roof onto the roof supports. Repeat to make 3 more mini gingerbread houses. Let icing stand overnight to harden.

4. Decorate gingerbread houses as desired, using a variety of candies and canned white icing.

Chocolate-Glazed Cookies

Prep 20 minutes   Stand 1 hour
Makes 16 cookies

1   bag (11.5-ounce) semisweet chocolate chips, *Ghirardelli®*
⅔   cup whipping cream
1   tablespoon light-color corn syrup, *Karo®*
2   bags (8.6 ounces each) large sugar cookies (16 cookies),
     Pepperidge Farms® Soft Baked
16   assorted chocolate candies

1. Place a wire rack on top of a baking sheet.

2. Place chocolate chips in a medium bowl; set aside. In a small saucepan, combine whipping cream and corn syrup; cook over medium heat just until boiling. Pour over chocolate chips; using a rubber spatula, stir until smooth.

3. Spread chocolate mixture on one side of a sugar cookie and place on wire rack, chocolate side up. Press a chocolate candy into the center of chocolate-glazed cookie. Repeat with the remaining cookies, chocolate mixture, and chocolate candies. Let stand about 1 hour or until chocolate hardens.

Bars and Bites

1. Go bananas. Peel and freeze ripe bananas, instead of throwing them away. They'll keep up to three months in freezer bags and can be thawed quickly to add flavor to chocolate, peanut butter, or fruit bars, or banana bread or cake.

2. Perfect cut. Slice brownies and bars with a pizza cutter—it's easier and the edges come out cleaner. Cut them into creative shapes, such as rectangles or diamonds.

3. A la mode. Turn bars into a complete dessert by serving with a scoop of ice cream or a spoonful of sweetened whipped cream. Fancy up brownies by sprinkling with powdered sugar, cocoa powder, or drizzling with a powdered sugar glaze.

4. A little nutty. When a recipe calls for peanut butter, use chunky peanut butter to add peanut butter and nuts in one quick step.

5. Lime over lemon. To give lemon squares an extra kick of flavor, substitute a little bit of lime juice for lemon juice.

The Recipes

Lemon Tart Squares

Prep 15 minutes **Bake** 15 minutes
Chill 3 hours **Makes** 16 squares

Nonstick vegetable cooking spray, *Pam*®
1 package (10-ounce) shortbread cookies, *Lorna Doone*®
1 tablespoon shredded lemon zest
1 stick (½ cup) butter, melted
½ cup lemon curd, *Dickinson's*®
1 can (15.75-ounce) lemon pie filling, *Comstock*® or *Wilderness*®
   Juice from lemon used for zest
   Powdered sugar (optional)

1. Preheat oven to 350 degrees F. Spray an 8-inch square baking pan with cooking spray. In a food processor, combine shortbread cookies and half of the lemon zest; cover and process until fine crumbs form. Add butter; pulse until mixture comes together. Press into prepared baking pan. Bake in preheated oven for 15 to 20 minutes or until golden brown. Cool in pan on wire rack.

2. Spoon lemon curd into a small microwave-safe bowl; microwave on high setting (100 percent power) about 30 seconds or until warmed. Stir until smooth. In a large bowl, stir together heated lemon curd, lemon pie filling, lemon juice, and the remaining lemon zest until well mixed. Pour over cooled shortbread crust.

3. Cover with plastic wrap and chill in refrigerator for 3 hours. Cut into squares. Sprinkle with powdered sugar just before serving (optional).

Key Lime Bars

Prep 15 minutes **Bake** 30 minutes
Makes 12 bars

3 cups coconut cookies, *Mother's Cookies*® *Cocadas*®
14 shortbread cookies, *Lorna Doone*®
½ cup pecans, *Planters*®
1 stick (½ cup) butter, melted
4 egg yolks
2¼ cups sweetened condensed milk, *Eagle Brand*®
¾ cup key lime juice, *Nellie & Joe's*®
½ cup lime curd, *Dickinson's*®
3 or 4 drops green food coloring, *McCormick*®

1. Preheat oven to 325 degrees F. In a food processor, combine coconut cookies, shortbread cookies, and pecans; cover and process until fine crumbs form. Add butter; pulse until mixture comes together. Press into 9-inch square baking pan.

2. In a large bowl, combine yolks, sweetened condensed milk, lime juice, lime curd, and green food coloring; beat with an electric mixer on low speed about 30 seconds or until well mixed. Pour over cookie crust. Bake in preheated oven for 30 to 35 minutes or until set. Cool to room temperature. Chill in refrigerator until completely cool. Cut into bars. Garnish with shredded *lime peel* (optional).

Strawberry Oat Squares

Prep 15 minutes   **Bake** 35 minutes
Makes 9 squares

1	pouch (17.5-ounce) oatmeal cookie mix, *Betty Crocker®*
1	stick (½ cup) butter, melted
1	can (21-ounce) strawberry pie filling, *Comstock® More Fruit*
1	cup frozen unsweetened strawberries, thawed, *Dole®*
2	teaspoons cornstarch
1	cup granola cereal, *Quaker® Oats & Honey*
½	cup sliced almonds, *Planters®*

1. Preheat oven to 375 degrees F. In a medium bowl, combine oatmeal cookie mix and melted butter, stirring with a wooden spoon until mixture comes together. Press into bottom of an 8-inch tart pan.

2. In a small bowl, stir together strawberry pie filling, strawberries, and cornstarch until combined. Pour strawberry mixture onto oatmeal crust, leaving a ¼-inch edge around sides. Sprinkle granola and almonds over top. Bake in preheated oven for 35 to 40 minutes or until bubbly around edges. Cool in pan on wire rack. Cut into wedges.

Linzer Bars

Prep 20 minutes   **Bake** 28 minutes
Makes 12 bars

	Nonstick vegetable cooking spray, *Pam®*
1	package (18.25-ounce) spice cake mix, *Betty Crocker®*
½	cup chopped hazelnuts (filberts), ground, *Diamond®*
1	stick (½ cup) butter, softened
1	tablespoon unsweetened cocoa powder, *Hershey's®*
1	egg
1	jar (10-ounce) raspberry jam, *Smucker's® Simply Fruit®*
½	cup pistachios, finely chopped, *Planters®*

1. Preheat oven to 350 degrees F. Spray a 9×13-inch baking pan with cooking spray and set aside.

2. In a large bowl, combine cake mix, ground hazelnuts, butter, cocoa powder, and egg; beat with an electric mixer on low speed until well mixed. Spread into prepared baking pan. Bake in preheated oven for 20 minutes.

3. Remove pan from oven; spread an even layer of raspberry jam over partially baked cake. Sprinkle pistachios on top. Bake for 8 to 12 minutes more or until wooden pick inserted in center of cake comes out clean.

4. Cool in pan on wire rack. Cut into bars.

Banana-Date Toffee Bars

Prep 15 minutes　　**Bake** 30 minutes
Makes 12 bars

Nonstick vegetable cooking spray, *Pam*®
2　eggs
½　cup vegetable oil, *Crisco*®
1　package (18.25-ounce) banana cake mix, *Duncan Hines*®
½　cup packed brown sugar, *C&H*®
1　cup chopped dates, *Sunsweet*®
½　cup chopped walnuts, *Planters*®
1　cup toffee bits, *Heath*®

1. Preheat oven to 375 degrees F. Spray a 9×13-inch baking pan with cooking spray.

2. In a large bowl, combine eggs and oil; beat with an electric mixer on low speed until smooth. Add cake mix and brown sugar. Beat on low speed until batter comes together like a soft dough. Stir in dates and walnuts until well mixed.

3. Spread dough into prepared baking pan. Sprinkle toffee bits over top; press gently into dough. Bake in preheated oven for 30 to 35 minutes or until set in center. Cool in pan on wire rack. Cut into bars.

Butterscotch-Cream Cheese Swirl Brownies

Prep 20 minutes　　**Bake** 40 minutes
Makes 12 brownies

Nonstick spray for baking, *Pam*®
1　package (18.3-ounce) fudge brownie mix, *Betty Crocker*®
⅔　cup vegetable oil, *Crisco*®
¼　cup low-fat chocolate milk, *Nesquik*®
3　eggs
1　cup butterscotch chips, *Nestlé*®
1　package (8-ounce) cream cheese, softened, *Philadelphia*®
3　tablespoons all-purpose flour, sifted
¼　cup butterscotch and caramel topping, *Mrs. Richardson's*®

1. Preheat oven to 350 degrees F. Spray a 9×13 glass baking dish with nonstick spray for baking and set aside.

2. In a large bowl, combine brownie mix, oil, chocolate milk, and 2 of the eggs, stirring with a wooden spoon until well mixed. Stir in butterscotch chips. Pour into prepared baking dish and set aside.

3. In a medium bowl, combine cream cheese and the remaining egg; beat with an electric mixer on low speed until smooth. Add flour; beat until combined. Stir in butterscotch and caramel topping. Drop spoonfuls of the cream cheese mixture into brownie batter. Using a butter knife, swirl cream cheese mixture into brownie batter for a marble effect. Bake in preheated oven for 40 to 45 minutes or until set. Cool in baking dish on a wire rack. Cut into bars.

Espresso Brownie Buttons

Prep 25 minutes   **Bake** 16 minutes
Cool 5 minutes   **Makes** 36 buttons

	Nonstick vegetable cooking spray, *Pam*®
1	box (18.3-ounce) fudge brownie mix, *Betty Crocker*®
6	tablespoons plus 1 teaspoon dry Café Vienna coffee drink mix, *General Foods*®
1	package (4-serving-size) instant butterscotch pudding and pie filling, *Jell-O*®
⅔	cup vegetable oil, *Crisco*®
¼	cup plus 1 tablespoon milk
2	eggs
1	cup powdered sugar, sifted, *C&H*®
	Additional café Vienna coffee drink mix (optional)

1. Preheat oven to 350 degrees F. Spray thirty-six 1¾-inch muffin cups with cooking spray.

2. In a large bowl, combine brownie mix, 6 tablespoons dry coffee drink mix, and the dry pudding mix. Add oil, ¼ cup milk, and eggs, stirring with a wooden spoon until well mixed. Scoop 1 tablespoon of the mixture into each muffin cup. Bake in preheated oven for 16 to 20 minutes or until brownies begin to pull from the sides of the pan.

3. Cool in pans on wire racks for 5 minutes. Carefully remove from muffin cups; cool on wire racks.

4. In a small bowl, stir together powdered sugar, the remaining 1 teaspoon coffee drink mix, and the remaining 1 tablespoon milk. Remove brownies from muffin cups; spoon about 1 teaspoon of the glaze over each. Sprinkle with additional dry coffee drink mix (optional).

Cupcakes

1. Make it match. Use color-coordinated cupcake papers as part of the presentation.

2. Larger than life. Instead of a sheet cake, use tube frosting or a disposable pastry bag to script letters on individual cupcakes—one letter per cupcake—and arrange on a platter to spell out a message. Surround with plain cupcakes decorated with candy to make a border.

3. Flavor add-in. Thin frosting with fruit juice or coffee. Adding some of the morning's coffee to chocolate frosting—or white cranberry juice to vanilla—gives it a gourmet taste.

4. Frosting softener. If the frosting hardens before you're finished with it, microwave for 30 to 60 seconds to soften. (Make sure you use a microwave-safe bowl.)

5. Beautiful finishes. Pair unusual toppings and contrast colors for a hint of the exotic. A kumquat looks sunny on lemon frosting, pistachios pop against chocolate, a sprig of lavender looks lovely against vanilla.

The Recipes

Banana Chip Cupcakes

Prep 20 minutes   Bake 20 minutes
Makes 12 large cupcakes

BANANA CHIP CUPCAKES:
1   package (18.25-ounce) banana cake mix, *Duncan Hines*®
1⅓   cups evaporated milk, *Carnation*®
¾   cup mashed bananas
¼   cup canola oil
2   eggs
¾   cup miniature chocolate chips, *Nestlé*®
½   cup toffee bits, *Heath*®
1   teaspoon banana extract, *McCormick*®
1   can (12-ounce) whipped chocolate frosting, *Betty Crocker*®

MONKEY FACES:
12   peanut butter sandwich cookies, *Nutter Butter*®
12   vanilla wafer cookies, *Nilla*®
    Black decorating icing, *Betty Crocker*®
24   rainbow-colored candies, *Skittles*®
    Chocolate sprinkles, *Betty Crocker*®

1. For Banana Chip Cupcakes, preheat oven to 350 degrees F. Line twelve large 3½-inch muffin cups with paper baking cups; set aside.

2. In a large bowl, combine cake mix, evaporated milk, mashed bananas, oil, and eggs; beat with an electric mixer on low speed for 30 seconds. Using a rubber spatula, scrape down side of the bowl and beat on medium speed for 2 minutes more. Stir in chocolate chips and toffee bits. Spoon about ¾ cup batter into prepared muffin cups, filling each about two-thirds full.

3. Bake for 20 to 25 minutes or until wooden pick inserted in centers comes out clean. Remove from muffin cups; place on wire racks and let cool. Stir banana extract into chocolate frosting; spread over cooled cupcakes.

4. For Monkey Faces, cut each peanut butter sandwich cookie in half crosswise (24 pieces total). Cut about one-quarter off the top of each vanilla wafer. For each cupcake, place 2 of the sandwich cookie pieces on a frosted cupcake, placing pieces toward top and across from each other. Add a vanilla wafer half between the sandwich cookie pieces, placing it slightly lower than the sandwich cookie pieces. Using black icing, pipe 2 small dots at the top of the vanilla wafer piece for nostrils. Pipe a smile with black decorating icing. For eyes, place 2 rainbow-colored candies above the vanilla wafer piece; pipe a dot of black icing in the middle of each candy piece. Sprinkle chocolate sprinkles above eyes for hair.

NOTE: To make regular-size cupcakes, line twenty-four 2½-inch muffin cups with paper baking cups. Continue as directed, except bake for 16 to 21 minutes and double all of the monkey face ingredients. (Makes about 24 cupcakes)

Cookies

1. Save some dough. Mix your dough ahead of time and refrigerate in an airtight container—when you're ready to bake, the prep is almost done. Dough keeps for up to two days in the refrigerator or up to three months in the freezer. Thaw frozen dough in the refrigerator until it's soft enough to use.

2. Clean-cut cookies. Spray cookie cutters with a nonstick cooking spray like Pam® to get a cleaner cut.

3. Try this. Create your own chocolate chip cookies by crumbling candy bars and swapping them for chocolate chips. Butterfinger®, Mounds® and Heath® bars all add fun and delicious flavors.

4. Add fruit. Give oatmeal cookies a color infusion by swapping chopped dried apricots, cherries, or Craisins® for raisins.

5. Big batch baking. If you're baking in batches, use multiple cookie sheets lined with parchment paper. When the first batch is done, the next batch is prepped and ready to slide in the oven.

The Recipes

Palm Leaves

Prep 30 minutes   **Bake** 20 minutes per batch
Chill 30 minutes   **Makes** 16 (2½-inch) pastries

½   **cup sweetened flaked coconut,** *Baker's*®
¼   **cup packed brown sugar,** *C&H*®
2   **teaspoons ground cinnamon,** *McCormick*®
1   **sheet frozen puff pastry dough, thawed,** *Pepperidge Farm*®
2   **tablespoons coarse sugar**

1. Preheat oven to 375 degrees F. Spread a thin, even layer of the coconut on a baking sheet. Bake in preheated oven about 10 minutes or until coconut is lightly toasted. Remove from baking sheet and cool completely.

2. In a small bowl, stir together toasted coconut, brown sugar, and cinnamon. Sprinkle 1 tablespoon of the coconut mixture on a flat working surface. Unroll puff pastry onto the working surface. Sprinkle the remaining coconut mixture evenly over puff pastry. Fold top and bottom edges of the puff pastry to the center. Fold pastry in half from left to right. Fold in half again from top to bottom. Place on an ungreased baking sheet and chill in refrigerator for at least 30 minutes.

3. Preheat oven to 400 degrees F. Line 2 cookie sheets with parchment paper and set aside.

4. Pour coarse sugar into a pie plate. Cut chilled dough into ½-inch-thick slices. Dip one side of a dough slice into sugar and place on prepared cookie sheet, sugar side up. Repeat with remaining slices, spacing 2 inches apart.

5. Bake in preheated oven for 20 to 22 minutes or until lightly browned and slightly puffed. Transfer to wire rack; serve warm or cool to room temperature.

Blueberry Cookie Torte

Prep 15 minutes **Bake** 13 minutes
Makes 8 servings

1	lemon
1	pouch (17.5-ounce) sugar cookie mix, *Betty Crocker®*
½	teaspoon baking powder
2	eggs
½	stick (¼ cup) butter, melted
1	package (8-ounce) cream cheese, *Philadelphia®*
1	container (8-ounce) frozen whipped topping, thawed, *Cool Whip®*
12	ounces fresh blueberries
¼	cup blueberry preserves, melted, *Dickinson's®*

1. Preheat oven 350 degrees F. Line a jelly-roll pan with parchment paper. Finely shred zest from lemon (if desired, reserve ½ teaspoon zest for garnish); squeeze ¼ cup juice from lemon. In a large bowl, combine cookie mix and baking powder. Add eggs, butter, the lemon zest, and the ¼ cup lemon juice; stir until well mixed. Pour into prepared pan. Bake in preheated oven for 13 to 15 minutes or until set in center. Let cookie cool in pan on wire rack. In a bowl, beat cream cheese with an electric mixer on low speed until smooth. Add whipped topping, stirring until combined.

2. Remove cookie from pan; peel off parchment. Cut cookie crosswise into thirds and place one cookie piece on a long serving plate. Top with one-third of the cream cheese mixture; top with one-third of the blueberries. Drizzle with one-half of the blueberry preserves. Repeat layers once, using remaining preserves. For the third layer, add last cookie piece to torte. Spoon remaining cream cheese mixture on cookie. Top with remaining blueberries. Garnish with reserved lemon zest (optional).

Cookie Pizza

Prep 25 minutes **Bake** 24 minutes
Makes 8 servings

1	pouch (17.5-ounce) peanut butter cookie mix, *Betty Crocker®*
3	tablespoons vegetable oil, *Crisco®*
1	tablespoon milk
1	egg
¾	cup white baking chips, *Nestlé®*
1	tube (6-ounce) red decorating icing, *DecACake®*
	Orange or yellow decorating icing, *Betty Crocker® Easy Flow*
	Assorted candy (such as fruit snacks and black gummy rings)

1. Preheat oven to 350 degrees F. Line a cookie sheet with parchment paper. In a bowl, stir together cookie mix, oil, milk, and egg until dough forms. Roll dough into a ball; pat out into an 11-inch circle. Place on prepared cookie sheet. Bake for 24 to 26 minutes or until set. Cool slightly on cookie sheet. Transfer cookie on paper to a wire rack; let cool.

2. Microwave white baking chips on medium setting (50 percent power) for 2 minutes or until melted, stirring every 30 seconds. Place cooled cookie on a plate. Spread red icing in a ring around cookie, leaving a 1½-inch border around edge. Spread melted white chips in the center of cookie to red icing border. Pipe yellow icing in strips to look like shredded cheese. Arrange assorted candies on cookie to look like pizza toppings.

Parties

1. Doll it up with doilies. Make any cookie tea party perfect with a fluted cookie cutter. Dress up the presentation by serving on a lacy paper doily.

2. Sophisticated sprinkle. Cut desired shapes in paper to use as a template. Sprinkle cocoa powder or powdered sugar on a plastic plate through template, then remove. Arrange a few sweets on top. It looks sophisticated, but the plates go straight in the trash.

3. Edible place card. Use readymade decorating icing to pipe each guest's monogram on a tart or cupcake. Set one at each place setting to double as dessert and place card.

4. Pudding bar. Open your own dessert bar by serving liqueur-flavored pudding or mousse in a martini glass with a pirouette garnish. They take just minutes to make with packaged ingredients.

5. Chocolate checkers. For a bit of whimsy, arrange squares of white and dark fudge or brownies in a checkerboard pattern. It'll really pop on a red plate with a raspberry garnish.

The Parties

Snowy Dessert Buffet

The holidays, a winter birthday, or a playful afternoon making snowmen are all reason to celebrate. Here's how: Deck your table in icy whites, silvers, and blues, turn powdered sugar donuts into a forest of frosted snowmen and dashing reindeer, and you've set the stage for a wonderful winter party.

Tablescape: The cool colors of winter provide the inspiration for a snowy-looking buffet table. Purchased foam cones become tabletop trees, covered with canned frosting and white powdered sugar donuts. Marshmallow snowmen rest candy cane skis on coconut-decked graham crackers for a touch of whimsy. Tiers of treats, shiny ornaments in glass vases, and icy blue candles on willowy candlesticks complete the winter wonderland.

Quick-scratch Christmas desserts: Cute-as-a-button snowmen get dressed for winter with white icing and edible blue accessories. Use cookie cutters to cut purchased sugar cookie dough into snowmen shapes, then get creative with canned frosting and candy embellishments. Decorations of candies, sprinkles, white chocolate-covered pretzels, and marshmallows give bakery-bought cupcakes an extra helping of holiday cheer.

April Showers

Welcome spring with a splash of bright colors and clever ideas. A happy palette of hot pink, lime green, and soft purple is perfect for any warm weather party—Mother's Day, a baby or bridal shower, or just the celebration of spring's arrival. Make it fun with gorgeous flowers, a sweet cake, and cocktails for everyone.

Tablescape: Rain boots in plaids and prints hold bouquets of sun-kissed flowers for easy centerpieces. Flowers of all kinds (but all in the same hues) make the table rich with color and texture. A plaid tablecloth repeats the spring-like theme while an open good-luck umbrella adds a punch of pink.

Cake and cocktails: A store-bought cake makes a quick party dessert on top of an inverted aluminum pie pan. Give the vanilla frosting a citrus boost with a hint of lemon extract, then add floral flourishes with colored tube frosting in pretty pastels. Add a splash of vodka to cranberry juice and serve in glasses for a one-minute cocktail.

Place cards and party favors: A lime green parchment envelope makes a clever easel for a computer-printed place card. Stack matching green-bordered plates on fuchsia chargers and color-coordinate flatware and glasses, keeping it all acrylic.

Glamorous Birthday

Add all-girl glamour to a special day with chic pinks in every shade, from rosebud to cherry. Then add just a hint of glossy black and the party becomes fashionably retro for any age and occasion, from "Sweet 16" to "It's a Girl"! Vintage-style dishes, nostalgia food, and classic cocktails are must-haves for the table.

Tablescape: Go glam with pink and black novelty dishes layered over a pink checkerboard cloth and fabric runners in pink stripes and a fun fashion toile. Make a beautiful cake candle the centerpiece, elevated on a black cake pedestal. Surround the cake with feathery pompoms and flank with bunches of ruffled pink blossoms in square black vases. Fill old-fashioned soda glasses with pink chocolate candies for a sweet surprise.

Food and drink: Store-bought cupcakes become the center of attention with pink-tinted frosting and a sweet cherry garnish. Serve virgin cocktails made with lemon-lime soda and grenadine syrup. For extra pizzazz use sugar-rimmed glasses and finish with a heart-shaped straw and cherry.
Party favors: A table sitter favor is always in vogue. Cut out and fold a black-on-pink silhouette to "sit" on the edge of the table at each plate. Add a pink feather boa for extra style.

Bright Berry Brunch

A soft spring breeze and the sweet scent of berries are the inspiration for a lovely old-fashioned brunch. A homey mix of strawberries, raspberries, and blueberries offer a colorful contrast, doubling as food and decor for a Mother's Day celebration, a bridal shower, or any time you feel like inviting a bunch for brunch.

Tablescape: Country colors take their cue from the berry patch. Cover the table in a berry print cloth, then create a simple centerpiece from a porcelain vase filled with clusters of faux strawberries and raspberries.

Place setting: Fruit-patterned dishes set a vintage tone, carried through to a red-striped dishtowel-turned-napkin tied with two-tone cording and tucked into a sweet berry bowl.

Food: Old-fashioned fruit tarts look like Grandma's but are much easier: Spoon mixed berries into purchased shells and brush the tops with warm honey for a tantalizing sparkle. Serve on a blue-rimmed glass cake pedestal.

Party favor: A place card is nested in a wicker bowl filled with speckled chocolate malt eggs. To make bird's nest favors for guests, cut a hanging tag out of berry print paper and tie it to the "nest" with a red ribbon.

Sweets for My Valentine

Rich browns and creamy whites set the mood for a sweet Valentine's party with chocolate as the central theme. Keep it supersimple yet stylish with bittersweet bonbons, milk chocolate bars, and fluffy pudding parfaits that your guests will absolutely adore. You'll love how easy it is—just buy, arrange, and serve!

Tablescape: A damask tablecloth in deep, dark shades of chocolate brings romance to the table. Chocolates are the main attraction, so take a tip from the candy store and show off your own assortment in curvy glass urns and clear vases stacked on cake plates.

Food and drink: Parfaits make for a stunning presentation but are so simple to make: Layer purchased vanilla and chocolate pudding in goblets and garnish with chocolate curls. Arrange purchased confections on decorative cake pedestals, topped with footed vases filed with scoop-it-yourself candies. Pair with a deep liqueur or brandy or serve white and black Russians to bring out the full flavors of each chocolate bite.

Place setting: Guide guests to their seats with personalized jumbo-size candy bars that go home as favors. Keep to the color scheme with brown-and-white floral dessert plates and matching bowls with a surprise monogram scripted on the bottom.

Midnight Sweet Soiree

Strike a chord that everyone will adore with a party that fits so many occasions. Classic black and white is so apropos for an after-theater gathering, a recital celebration, or a milestone birthday. Glowing candles show off the soft sheens of silver and gold for an evening that starts off on the right note.

Tablescape: A metallic silver-on-black tablecloth is a refined backdrop for swagged black beaded candelabras and mercury glass candlesticks. Increase the sparkle with glass plates, black goblets, and ornate silverware. Rolled and tied sheets of music add to the theme while gold votive candles in bubble glass holders cast a romantic moon-like glow over each elegant black-and-white place setting.

Food and drink: Pears poached in red wine add texture and color to the table. For a party-perfect presentation, serve them in a swirled glass wine goblet over a rich, creamy white chocolate mousse or French vanilla pudding, swizzled with a bit of the poaching liquid from the pear. A strawberry martini is the picture of understated elegance in a simple short-stemmed martini glass.

Place cards: A personal note makes a thoughtful keepsake place card. Fold pieces of black-and-white scrapbook paper in half and jot a warm welcome inside of each—such as a personalized message to each guest, a short poem, or an inspiring thought for the day. Glue an elegant scripted place card to the front of each message card. For a final flourish, thread black satin ribbons through the hole-punched tops and gently tie them around pages of rolled-up sheet music.

Denim and Diamonds

A little bit of country and a lot of city chic make for a hip party any time of year. Soft denim blues and homespun calicos play off crystal and rhinestones to create a feeling of relaxed elegance—just the mood for celebrating a casual birthday, an after-the-horse-race party, or an engagement announcement.

Tablescape: Rhinestones and clear glass accessories glisten against a rough-and-tumble denim tablecloth cut straight from the bolt. Carry through the blues with glued-down denim silverware pockets and stacked calico and denim dinnerware encircled with a faux crystal "necklace." Roll up denim napkins and add a silver clasp with a glued-on crystal bauble.

Drink: A white diamond milkshake looks oh-so-country but tastes undeniably rich with those backyard burgers. Blend vanilla ice cream, milk, and pure vanilla extract and pour it into an retro milkshake glass finished with a blue straw for sipping.

Window treatment: For no-sew shades, cover a purchased window shade with denim fabric and hot-glue darker denim pockets on top. Glue strands of faux crystal chandelier beading around the shade to complete your denim and diamonds look.

Birthday Science Project

This science-minded party is sure to earn you an "A" for awesome. A kaleidoscope of crazy colors and cool toy store favors will make your next kids' party the hit of the neighborhood. Add a smokin' volcano cake and fizzy test tube punch, and you've got all the mixins and fixins for a blowout birthday celebration.

Tablescape: A table full of bright-colored toys and candy says, "Let's party!" Fill a neon green colander with lollipops and stick candy to make a treat-yourself centerpiece, surrounded by take-home toy favors. Keep it carefree with plastic plates and tumblers in a playful confetti pattern, perfect with the pop art tablecloth.

Food and drink: Mixed with lemon-lime soda, fruit juice coolers bubble and fizz—just like a chemistry set.

Serve them in beaker-style glasses with colorful curly straws. To make a volcano cake, spread canned frosting between store-bought cakes stacked on a cutting board. Trim into a cone shape, cover with fudge frosting, and decorate with trails of lava-colored tube frosting. For a volcano eruption, hide a glass with a bit of dry ice in the well of the cake; when you're ready to serve, pour a little hot water into it for "smoke". Keep kids away from the ice!

Index

Index

Free
Lifestyle web magazine subscription

Just visit
www.semihomemade.com
today to subscribe!

Sign yourself and your friends and family up to the semi-homemaker's club today!

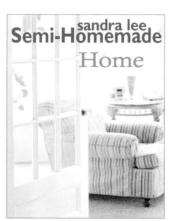

Each online issue is filled with fast, easy how-to projects, simple lifestyle solutions, and an abundance of helpful hints and terrific tips. It's the complete go-to magazine for busy people on-the-move.

tables & settings	fashion & beauty	ideas	home & garden	fabulous florals
super suppers	perfect parties	great gatherings		decadent desserts
gifts & giving	details	wines & music	fun favors	semi-homemaker's club

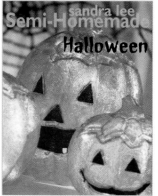

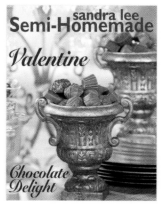

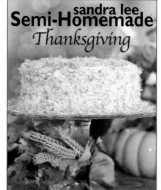

semihomemade.com

making life easier, better, and more enjoyable

Semihomemade.com has hundreds of ways to simplify your life—the easy Semi-Homemade way! You'll find fast ways to de-clutter, try your hand at clever crafts, create terrific tablescapes or decorate indoors and out to make your home and garden superb with style.

We're especially proud of our Semi-Homemakers club: a part of semihomemade.com which hosts other semihomemakers just like you. The club community shares ideas to make life easier, better, and more manageable with smart tips and hints allowing you time to do what you want! Sign-up and join today—it's free—and sign up your friends and family, too! It's easy the Semi-Homemade way! Visit the site today and start enjoying your busy life!

Sign yourself and your friends and family up to the semi-homemaker's club today!

tablescapes   home   garden   organizing   crafts

everyday & special days   cooking   entertaining   cocktail time

Halloween   Thanksgiving   Christmas   Valentine's   Easter   New Year's

Collect all of Sandra's books

Save Money ◆ Create More Time ◆ Make Life Easier